# I AM A
# #REMAINERNOW

"To those who voted Leave, I am sorry I can't share your fight anymore

To those who voted Remain, I am sorry I contributed to this mess

And to those who have changed their minds about Brexit, remember that you are not alone and that you are among some of the bravest people I have had the privilege in knowing"

- CHRISTOPHER ORAM

**Part 1**
**The officials**

**Part 2**
**RemainerNow Stories**

**Part 3**
**RemainerNow Articles from 'Politics Means Politics' website**

## Part 4
## Moving Forward

**PART ONE**
**The Officials**

**A foreword from Andy, the founder of the RemainerNow movement**

Looking Back

I'm not a political activist, but for 2 years from the 15th December 2017, I became one in my spare time, when I was driven to start a twitter account called @RemainerNow.

My first tweet read: "There is a lot of evidence that public opinion is turning against #Brexit - many people who voted #leave in #EUREF regret their decision now the facts are clear. This account has been set up to share stories of those who are #Remainernow & have been brave enough to say!"

I did not know what to expect when I started it. I did not know if anyone would even pick up on it. However, in the first few weeks it grew rapidly. I gained new followers at a rate of about 100 a day, many of who were active in liking, retweeting and replying to the stories I shared of those EU Referendum Leave voters who had boldly come out and said that, now they have seen the way Brexit is going and what it may mean for the UK, they were a #RemainerNow. Those who wanted to say it's ok to change your mind and wanted Brexit to stop, by way of another public vote on the reality of Brexit or otherwise.

Three months on and my little account (thanks to the help of others that started coming on board) had grown into a full-fledged campaign. In the weeks and months that followed this initiative expanded even more. We had started a Facebook group to reach new audience, then a website (www.remainernow.com) and later Instagram and we had YouTube accounts. All these were designed to celebrate those people who, when faced with what was often an ugly and divisive issue, were willing to say 'it's ok to change my mind' and let many others who felt the same were not alone. The hope was to turn the tide and push back.

Up until the December 2019 General Election we were very active and did many things on top of our social media platforms. With the help of those who donated to our crowdfunds, we planned events such as group campaign visits to both Parliament in Westminster and Brussels to share #RemainerNow stories with politicians, we attended 3 different party conferences in 2019, we organized #RemainerNow groups to march together and speak at

1

various anti-brexit rallies throughout the country, we worked with local anti Brexit groups to help their efforts, and we commissioned videos for people to tell their stories. We also did what we could to help those regretful leavers who wanted to share get their stories to press. The hope was that all these steps would encourage others who felt that, now they have seen how the Government has interpreted (or misinterpreted) their leave vote, and have seen where the country is headed, to speak out and add their voices to those already saying they want the UK to change course. We hoped that it would help those politicians who felt Brexit was wrong for the UK to not feel they had to follow the 2016 brexit referendum had to be followed.

Sadly in the end, despite the fact that for over 2 years up to and including the 2019 General Election, nearly every single poll that asked how the public would vote if the EU referendum question was asked again indicated the answer would have been different, Brexit became inevitable and unstoppable. If we had got that "People's Vote" in late 2019 or early 2020 (like for a long time it looked like we would) we hoped that this (very much grassroots) campaign could have had influence on the result, but it was not to be.

I would like to thank Chris for putting together this book which gives just a small sample of some of the views of those people who changed their views on Brexit and became #RemainerNow over the 3 and a half years that followed. When he started it in late 2019 it was at a time when Brexit was anything but inevitable, but now these stories are a great representation of a key aspect of democracy, that its ok to change your mind.

The rest of this section is a copy of something I wrote right at the start of the campaign back in early 2018. It was written to respond to questions I had received from those who supported what I was doing. I am not, and never was the story here and for much of the campaign I stayed anonymous. However, it was felt that people knowing some background and my motivation for doing what I was doing would make people feel more able or more comfortable to contribute. It's a tiny bit out of date now but its been included as it may be of interest to some. If I is then, please continuing reading here, if not, please turn to the main #RemainerNow stories, which are a sample of the personal accounts that made the campaign what it was.

## Am I a #Remainernow myself?

In short, no, I voted Remain and, if I am honest, I never even considered voting Leave.

Whilst recognising it is not in any way perfect, and most certainly needs some reform, I have always been pro-EU.

This was primarily because:

a. Peace - As a keen historian (up to A-level anyway) I recognise the EU's importance as a peace project.

b. Economics - As part of a wider A-level economics trip to London in 2002 I attended a talk on the EU by Ken Clarke MP. He talked passionately about the benefits of free trade and regulatory alignment with our nearest neighbours and this stuck with me & has only grown since.

And there are so many other reasons I am more pro EU/anti-Brexit now than I was even at the time of the vote, such as the horrific uncertainty for all the EU citizens (who add so much to this country), the terrible mess about what Brexit means for the Irish border, or the fact the Government and Parliament can't really deal with anything else but Brexit... but these above were my two main reasons at the time.

Was I political before?

No, not before David Cameron announced the EU Referendum in February 2016. I had always voted in General Elections and, if I was able, local and EU elections, and I was interested in things like constitutional & electoral reform from some of my studies, but that was about it.

That all changed when the EU Referendum was called, when, due to my long-held views of the benefits of the EU, I suddenly became much more interested. I followed the campaigns closely, I watched the debates and I shared various articles on Facebook etc. But, I'm ashamed to say, didn't campaign at all. This was partly for personal reasons (my first child was born in March 2016 so much of my spare time was spent enjoying time with her, and helping my wife) but it was also because I did not think I needed to. Maybe it was due to being a 31-year-old working in London where nearly all my peers were Remainers, but I never thought for one-second that the referendum would result in a Leave vote. Out of the people I did speak to during the campaigns, only 2 or 3 were planning to vote Leave and these were for long-held ideological reasons regarding sovereignty.

I thought it would only be people like them, and far right UKIP supporters, that would vote Leave. (Don't get me wrong, I thought the Remain campaign was poor. It failed to properly publicise all of benefits that EU membership brings us, and things like the threat of a 'punishment budget' lacked

3

credibility and distracted from the more truthful predictions). Nevertheless, I thought for everyone apart from these two groups, the economic evidence would win out, and Remain would sail through. I did not appreciate all of the other reasons why (that I more than appreciate now, and which I will return to later) so many people would feel their best option was voting Leave.

From dismayed citizen to activist.

Now onto the main reason I am disrupting my life and that of my young family by doing this, and why have I been spending so much of my limited free time over the past months running an anonymous twitter account seeking out #bregretter; the Brexit Regretters.

I hope what follows will resonate with some, and if it encourages even just a handful of people who feel like me to increase efforts or, more importantly, if it encourages a number of #bregretters to step forward and speak out, it is certainly worth it.

As I explained above, I never thought the UK was in danger of voting to leave the EU, I was in fact on holiday that week with my wife and 3-month-old (both of us having sent off postal votes the week before). When the result was announced, I was in complete shock and the last two days of my holiday, totally ruined.

I couldn't understand it. How could the UK vote against its economic security?
I did not to know what to think of the 17.4 million leave voters. Were they all ideologues like my two friends? Was it a lack of understanding?

Were they racist? I am ashamed to say I did a couple of emotive Facebook posts to that effect in the early hours of 24 June when I turned on the radio and heard the results coming through, and I apologise for that. I honestly feared what all this would mean for my daughter's future and our country. However, when I returned to work the next Monday I came across my first Brexit regretter (#bregretter), someone I was working with at the time.

We were out for lunch with a 16-year-old work experience student and the conversation inevitably turned to the referendum. I could not hide my despair at the whole situation! To my surprise my colleague explained that she voted leave on the spur of the moment in the booth because (a) she'd always voted Labour so wanted to vote against the Tory PM; and (b) her friends were voting leave for the same reason. She told me she instantly regretted it the next morning when she saw the chaos; she had just wanted to protest!

This opened my eyes a fair bit, and I quickly started to realise that many leave voters probably didn't have the UKIP view of Britain I had feared. So, I found that my anger had turned away from the voters, and towards the politicians that had misled them, often for their own personal gain (Boris Johnson was attempting to be PM – for the first time).

Although I did not do any proper anti-Brexit campaigning at the start (for various reasons including family ones), over the summer of 2016, which I now see as being vital, I started educating myself about why the leave vote happened. I read lots of articles on the topic when I came across them on twitter etc. I remember watching a programme with Adrian Chiles called "Why we voted Leave". Again, this opened my eyes to the fact many 'leavers' had completely understandable reasons for their vote against the status quo and I completely empathised with them. I mainly stayed angry at the politicians who advocated it.

I continued to follow Brexit closely. I was disgusted by May's 'citizens of nowhere' speech at the party conference in the autumn of 2016. I was dismayed when, in March 2017, after the Miller case gave MPs the chance to do their jobs and act in their constituents best interests, all but a few honourable MPs waved through the Article 50 legislation almost unchallenged.

When Theresa May called the 2017 snap General Election requesting a mandate for her Brexit plan, I was petrified. May had proven over the prior 9 months that she was only listening to the Hard Right of her party, and the right wing press, rather than finding some common ground that also recognised both the wishes of the 48%, and those of "soft" leavers and would minimise the economic harm of Brexit.

I was convinced, with the polling as it was, the Conservatives would win a stonking majority and that would be it, the hardest of hard Brexits and all the economic pain and damage to international reputation that would come with it. Despite what I had going on with both work and family, I did my first ever on the ground political campaigning at the 2017 General Election for one of the parties which I had joined the year before. I also did a bit on Twitter, and finally (like many others who felt like me) I spent a lot of time on the Pro-EU Facebook groups encouraging tactical voting and vote swaps. Anything I could think of to try and limit May's majority and thwart her imagined Hard Brexit mandate.

5

I was so happy when that exit poll came out and it looked like we were heading to a hung parliament.

I realised that there would now be a chance to #StopBrexit, or at least ensure Single Market membership was maintained. And for the first time, I felt I could change the outcome, that my voice mattered, maybe even more than my vote. This led to me upping my activism, but this still mainly involved me increasing the frequency of emailing my MP (which I had done for the first time in late June 2016), predominately about the key Brexit-related votes.

The tipping point and the start of a movement…

As I said above, ever since the Referendum, I had been interested in understanding the reasons why people voted Leave. I had also been noticing a gradually increasing number of people expressing Brexit regret on twitter. Their reasons varied: 'there would in fact be no money for the NHS,' 'it was all too complicated,' 'a multiple billion Euro divorce bill,' 'only voted leave on the basis that we would stay in the Single Market' (After all many leave politicians had advocated as such.)

I read them all with interest, but did not engage too much. Then, in the late summer and early autumn of 2017, I came across three Brexit regretters whose stories I found really interesting.

All three had started to speak out that they regretted their decision and were also actively campaigning against Brexit. I read their blogs/threads/letters to their MPs they had written explaining their reasons for voting Leave, and why they had changed their minds: Tim from the Midlands, Hugh from West-country and Simon from the North-West. I followed these three closely, and they gave me invaluable understanding to why so many people voted Leave and why these three, in particular now regretted their vote.

Reading their stories, and seeing how they interacted with other people about Brexit, got me thinking. I had not come across anyone trying to properly work with regretful leavers to encourage them to speak out and it turned out a few others had been collecting evidence, although I did not know this at the time.

The seed for @Remainernow was sown.

From November 2017, a number of things happened in a short period, that made me realise I had to do more than I had been, to fight what I believe is a complete and utter Brexit shambles which will severely damage the country I love.

The first thing to occur was Nick Clegg published a book called 'How to Stop Brexit (and Make Britain great Again)' and I dropped a hint to my wife about Christmas gift ideas. She instead bought it for me then and there, and I read it in a weekend. Some people now cringe when Nick Clegg's name is mentioned, but whatever you think of the Coalition, if you believe in fighting Brexit, give it a chance, and recognise the truth in what he has to say on this issue. For what it's worth, this point about Clegg, also applies to Tony Blair, even if you hate him for some, or many, of things he did in Government, you have to respect that in his recent interventions on Brexit he is on the money.

Indeed, the same applies to Ken Clarke and Michael Heseltine, whatever your thoughts of them in Government, the fact that they are publicly hammering Brexit as total folly should be championed!

This is a cross-party issue.

I found Clegg's book both inspiring and uplifting. After explaining why it is right and not undemocratic to stop Brexit he encourages people to get out there, join political parties and pro-EU groups.

That evening I signed up to my closest pro-EU group at the time, Islington In Europe, and ensured I was on the mailing lists for a number of national pro-EU groups (Best for Britain, Open Britain and European Movement – I had followed some of them for some time but only from a distance) to ensure I was aware what is going on, as I realised more needed to be done.

My next reason for doing more to fight at this particular point, was very personal. My wife and I had our 12 week scan for our 2nd child a few days later, I was obviously very excited, but I realised that, if Brexit goes ahead, and it harms the country as much as I fear, I want to be able to look both my kids in the eye when they are older and tell them I at least fought against it in an effort to protect their futures. I just needed to decide how best to do it.

Then in early December 2017 it was revealed that the serving Brexit Secretary, David Davis, had failed to do any impact assessments into what his department's Brexit plans would mean for the UK after an entire 16 months in office. I was absolutely livid.

In what other job can you make a huge decision like this without doing a cost benefit analysis of the different options? No business leader, doctor, or lawyer would act this way, and they are not making decisions that could affect the prosperity of an entire country for generations to come.

That evening, I started doing a bit of research on whether a criminal case could be brought against him for malfeasance in public office or perhaps a negligence claim for breach of duty? I didn't pursue these, as it seems the bar is quite high particularly for the criminal charge, so I will leave it to lawyers who are actually experts in the field to tackle. But what the anger did do was make me join my first ever political protest outside parliament on a freezing cold Monday night on 11th December 2017.

Whilst there I got chatting to two people who it turns out run anti-Brexit twitter accounts I had been following. These are @EUflagmafia & @wooferendum (please check them out to see the great things they are doing). I had really interesting chats with both of these guys about what they were doing, and their motivations, and was hugely inspired by them. This was yet another push to do something similar.

Finally, later that week I came across an exchange between two #RemainerNow ladies in response to a tweet from Martin Lewis, the 'Money Saving Expert,' about Brexit. A lady called Julie expressed her regret and stated that she felt her vote had been "formed on lies and deception and I don't like being fooled," and then a lady called Anne simply replied with, "Me too....grrr!"

It was Julie's tweet in reply, "If more people who feel like us... and I am certain there are many, felt able to speak out too, the numbers would be powerful" that was the final push. Julie had just stated in a tweet something I had been thinking for months, and that evening I started @RemainerNow with Julie's message being one of the first examples of Brexit regret I shared.

Just 3 months later, the account had in excess of 6,000 followers (now over 43000) including a number of MEPs, MPs and Journalists. It has helped enable like-minded Leave voters who have changed their minds and do not want Brexit to happen to connect, encourage each other and share their stories. And what's more, these #bregretters are finding themselves welcomed into a community of pro-EU people like myself, happy to learn more from their experiences.

I continue to come across a number of new Brexit regretters every day. So what now?

I read a piece in the New European newspaper a while ago, which said:

*"It's beyond time MPs stopped parroting this 'The People have spoken' nonsense and start instead to represent The People's interests. The vote of 23 June, 2016 was always about so much more than Membership of the European Union. George Osborne's austerity, trolleys in hospital corridors, an utter absence of social strategy, underinvestment in infrastructure, the size of our kid's classrooms, the queues at our GP."*

My experience over the previous summer following brexit regretters, and in these first months of 2018 when I have engaged with hundreds more, confirms that at least for a significant portion of Leave voters this holds true.

I know from conversing with so many people that there are a multitude of reasons why people voted to quit the EU, and over the coming series of articles/blogs, I will be sharing different stories every week to spotlight a few of these from the people who made those choices.

I believe Brexit must be stopped. But, it should not be stopped for or by people like me, or for the politicians speaking out for the cause. It should be stopped for people like Hugh, Simon, Tim, Julie, Josh, Emma, Chris, Dami, Luke and all of the other Leave voters who feel Brexit delivered will be nothing at all like the Brexit advertised. It should also be stopped for our kids and grandkids: those who will have to live the longest with its ramifications.

So for these people, my friends and family, present and future, I am not just going to run the @Remainernow twitter account and work to expand the initiative in the ways I explained at the start of this piece. I am doing all the things I encourage all #RemainerNow people to do. I have and will continue to join pro-EU groups for action days, making it clear that Brexit is not a done deal. I will continue to write letters to my MP.

The reasons so many voted Leave out of protest, disaffection and neglect are all still there, and must be dealt with. It's just that Brexit, in any form, as confirmed by the leaked government impact studies, will make all these far, far worse.

If anything I have said here resonates with you, either as a Leave voter with Brexit regret, or as a passionate Remain voter looking to support these people that speak out, please follow @Remainernow on our platforms or volunteer to help this campaign, and please above all, share your stories. As I have said before, your voices are the ones that can make the change I believe this country needs.

**Jamie Woodhouse**

https://jamiewoodhouse.com/

#RemainerNow voices are the most important in the Brexit debate. They show that the already questionable 2016 mandate has crumbled and they remind us of the benefits of EU membership and the damage that Brexit would cause. They're a refreshing, powerful contrast to the dull and often unproductive noise of the remain vs. leave debate. That's why I work to help them get heard. Leave voters are much more likely to listen to other leave voters than to boring remainers like me.

I'm often the first person to make contact with a potential RemainerNow given my volunteer role in the team. I check people's Twitter history (yes, this can be eye opening) but, more importantly, I talk to people to understand why they voted leave or abstained and what has led them to change their mind. Speaking out on this most divisive of topics takes bravery, so I connect people with the RemainerNow community early for support and advice. It's also important to check the integrity of people whose voices we amplify. Very occasionally I've come across a well-meaning remain voter who thinks pretending to have voted leave and changed their mind will help the cause. It doesn't.

It's been a real privilege to talk to hundreds of RemainerNow people. They come from all over the country, from every conceivable background and demographic – yet they are all intellectually honest, brave, and they want the best for the UK. For every one of them talking openly on social media, there are many more in the country at large. I hope they'll be heard. The 17.4 million is no longer.

So what makes someone change their mind about Brexit? There are many different reasons, so I've tried to give a flavour of them here. Every comment below has been made by at least one #RemainerNow I've spoken to personally. Some reasons are common to many. I keep this list updated here: https://jamiewoodhouse.com/remainernow-reasons. Please let me know @JamieWoodhouse if you hear of more. All credit is due to the #RemainerNow people who have told me their stories. Thank you all.

**Just #MakeItStop so we can focus on real UK problems**
"I just want it to be over (remaining is the only way)."

"Our government has already wasted 3 years on Brexit when so much needs fixing in the UK. If we go ahead with Brexit – government will be doing nothing else for another decade or more."

"I didn't realise how complex Brexit was going to be and how badly our government would mess it up. Even if we still want to leave we need to revoke Article 50 now and have another think."

"Brexit has made us an international embarrassment – staying in the EU is the best way of starting to rebuild our reputation."

## I voted in protest – at Cameron, at austerity, at my GE votes not counting

"Protest vote gone wrong – just wanted to give Cameron and the government / establishment a kicking – I didn't want this."

"I never thought leave could win – so was comfortable voting as a protest."

## Vote Leave promises have been broken

"The Brexit's on offer in 2019 are so different from 2016 promises (sunlit uplands, easiest deal ever)."

"Vote Leave promised we'd have a deal negotiated before triggering the legal process to leave. Now they're claiming we voted for no-deal!"

"I voted to leave because I thought we could pursue a more socialist agenda outside the EU. Now Brexit feels like a hard-right Tory project + I don't see the EU constraining other left-wing governments."

"I wanted an EFTA / Norway / Soft Brexit. Given those aren't on offer I'd prefer to remain. My vote seems to be being co-opted for ever harder versions of Brexit."

"I felt like we should respect the result of the 2016 referendum – but it promised something we now know is impossible."

"I believed we could get a deal that included all the benefits of EU membership without the constraints. I now know that was never realistic."

"The Leave campaign lied (NHS, Turkey, trade deals)."

"The Vote Leave campaign broke electoral law."

## Leave politicians / leaders don't represent me

"I'm disgusted with the people pushing Brexit – they don't share my values / I don't trust their motives."

"I'm shocked at the way our government is willing to even undermine democracy and the rule of law to make a no-deal Brexit happen. This isn't my Brexit."

"Brexit seems to have emboldened the far-right – I want no part of that."

**I see the EU in a different light now**
"Our politicians and press only ever talked about the negatives of the EU.
The benefits were hidden or claimed by UK politicians as their own.
I've learned so much more about the benefits of trade, international
co-operation, freedom of movement."

"I didn't like the idea of EU regulations being imposed on the UK – but
then I realised we're part of making those rules and none of them
negatively impact my life at all."

"I'd lost touch with the EU as couldn't really afford to travel – it just didn't
feel relevant. I've since visited EU countries with my family – it's
helped me feel more of a connection."

"Was told the EU was falling apart – now it seems stronger than ever."

"I'm nervous about the UK standing alone given behaviour of the US, Russia, China – re: trade and security issues."

"Given how global politics has shifted in the US, India, China, Turkey and
Russia – feels like the EU is the only powerful hope for liberal
democracy and we need to stay part of that."

"I thought we could strike trade deals with the US, China and Common-
wealth countries that would more than offset what we lose in EU trade
and that just doesn't seem realistic now."

"I still have criticisms of the EU, but the damage to the UK from leaving
isn't worth it – we should stay and help make things better."

"I voted to leave because I was worried about where the EU might be going.
Now I think it's better to stay and influence that direction. We can
always leave later if we fail and disagree."

"I voted to leave because I wanted the EU to be more directly democratic.
To actually take some power away from nation states and give it back
to the European people. Instead, Brexit now seems to be driven by the
nationalism I despise."

**"Project Fear" is becoming project reality**
"I've talked to my kids / grandkids and didn't realise how they felt about
Brexit's impact on jobs / rights / public services."

"Didn't think about UK people losing our freedom of movement rights
(live, work, retire in 31 countries)."

"Protecting The Union (Scotland + Northern Ireland) – I didn't even think
about Ireland in 2016 – Vote Leave didn't mention it."

"Fears over job losses – 'project fear' seems to be coming true."

"Worried about NHS staffing + funding."

"Concerned about availability of critical drug / medical supplies for me and
  my family."
"Worried trade will impact public services funding / tax take and lead to yet
  more self-imposed austerity."
"I've heard stories about the impact of Brexit on millions of EU people in
  the UK (e.g. stress of the settled status process) and UK people in the
  EU."

**Brexit won't help the UK regions**

"I voted leave partly to free the UK to invest more in the regions. Now I've
realised the EU care more about UK regions than Westminster does."
"I felt as though the benefits of EU membership all helped London, but
  didn't do much for the regions. Now I see that Brexit will cause most
  damage to the poorest regions."

### Christopher Oram - Shaftesbury, Dorset

## Cheated

One thing I have noticed above all other considerations whilst being a spokesperson and a podcast host for RemainerNow is how cheated everyone feels. The remainers feel cheated because they are being forced into a Brexit that will make our lives worse and not better. The leavers feel cheated because everything they were promised in 2016 cannot be delivered. Besides this, they continue to 'believe,' which ultimately will lead to more disappointment regardless of who or what influences the final conclusion.

However, I believe that the people who have been cheated the most are people like me. The leavers or the abstainers who have changed their minds about how they acted during the referendum. We now know we were lied to. We now know that Farage, Johnson and Gove are not the men we once thought they were. We now know the leave campaign was built upon lies, undeliverable promises, over-exaggerated flaws in the EU and even needed to break electoral law in order to win.

Despite knowing this, we who would style ourselves RemainerNows are being ignored. I find this most frustrating and cocoons me in a deep sense of being cheated. I am no longer a man of the leave camp, thrown out into the political desert because I had the audacity to question the leave manifesto when it didn't add up. The nerve to be upset with the leaders of the campaign when they made U-turns about their promises. The courage to stand up straight in this divisive situation and say: 'I was wrong'.

I was a leaver but by god this isn't what I wanted. This wasn't what I was promised. This was never the plan and this nonsense doesn't represent my vote. I am a Remainer-Now.

You may think that being a RemainerNow would give us a VIP ticket to all the Remainer rallies, but unfortunately that's not always the case. Sometimes we are welcomed with open arms and other times we are shunned or ignored. We are accused of not doing our homework the first time and that we deserve everything we get for putting people in this position. If the mainstream media was a little more sympathetic to our plight, we may have stood a better chance with being understood.

**Why did I vote Leave?**

People of all ages and backgrounds question my authenticity as a former Brexit voter and try to demoralise my argument by simply denying I ever voted for it.

A lot of people refuse to believe that someone would be swept up in the extra £350M per week pledge on the side of a bus. I did. It was my number one reason. You must understand that I wasn't politically active back in 2016. I didn't read the newspapers or watched the news every evening. I didn't go out of my way to understand politics and the way we do things in this country like I do now.

Most of my information was collected on social media which, when you look at it logically, is no way to encourage critical thinking. The people whose posts you see on a daily basis are usually your friends. Friends and close circles tend to have similar views on the world which by definition is an echo chamber. When a post about how we have to abide by laws passed over by a "bunch of unelected bureaucrats" enters your social circle, it is very difficult, or perhaps just laziness, to not take the information as gospel and challenge it with any serious thinking. You become a product of your own environment.

I was caught up in this cycle. My father is a Conservative voter and of the opinion that if you're living well under a government then don't try and change it. This argument came crashing down when the EU question was asked because my dad was a dairy farmer years ago and blames the EU quotas on milk for the death of his beloved industry. I sympathise with him of course, to a point.

My second biggest reason for voting leave was the depiction of immigrants coming into the country. I'm in no way xenophobic, but I was probably sharing social circles with people who secretly were. To no finer point, the argument I heard the most was that we were over-run, inundated and over-whelmed by people coming into the country. We blamed immigration for longer waits at hospitals and the modern struggle to get an appointment with the local GP. We presumed that this was why it was difficult to find work. All these arguments came to fruition when Nigel Farage stood in front of a 'breaking point' poster which depicted people of other races queuing up to enter the country. Soon after, phrases like 'getting our country back' and 'take back control' became mainstream.

Further to these two main points, I was also taken by the care-free way in which some leave campaigners spoke about the transition:

> *"The free Trade Agreement that we will do with the European Union should be one of the easiest in human history"* - Dr Liam Fox MP

> *"Absolutely nobody is talking about threatening our place in the single market"* - Daniel Hannan MEP

> *"We could be like Norway or Switzerland!"* - Nigel Farage

> *"The day after we vote to leave, we hold all the cards and we can choose the path we want."* - Michael Gove MP

> *"Taking back control is a careful change, not a sudden step - we will negotiate the terms of a new deal before we start any legal process to leave."* - Vote Leave campaign website

> *"Only a madman would leave the [single] market"* - Owen Patterson MP

I was under the impression that staying in the single market and customs union was would be the epicentre of our negotiations. With other influential speakers saying it would be easy and (essentially) risk free, I felt very little fear in giving my vote to the leave campaign.

Due to this, I already had a distrust of the EU. My family and social media was my whole political education. I was not qualified to make a decision on whether to leave or not. So when the referendum came around I was looking forward to voting for a United Kingdom Independence Day.

The Remain campaign didn't sell the benefits of EU; they only scare-mongered against leaving, which was later dubbed 'project fear.' The Leave camp sold positive messages and appealed to the emotional. A strong campaign which we should have seen from the start, was void of facts, full of undeliverable promises and comprising of mostly over-exaggerated short-falls in the European Union.

## Why did I change my mind?

April 3rd 2017 10:20 am - Cornwall

I had just finished a walk across the Tintagel cliffs and walked achingly back into the cottage I had rented for the week. I was alone, taking a week off to myself to find some writing inspiration and catch up on my Journalism diploma.

I had left the cottage early so I could get a long walk in before returning to my laptop for the remainder of the day. Many writers like writing in silence and some prefer some background noise. Some music, a busy road, the radio or even the news just to fill the silence. I am of the latter; so when I chose to turn on the Radio it started playing the last thing it was tuned into. In this case it was a Radio programme called LBC and the presenter was a man called James O'Brien.

James O'Brien was talking about the ridiculous notion of having blue passports. Inviting people to call in and explain exactly why that was considered a huge victory. I don't remember the conversation entirely but over the next few days I became totally spellbound by his relentlessness and no-nonsense attitude to the people calling his radio program. I quickly learned that trying to argue with this man was a futile assignment and instead, I contented myself in just listening to him ridicule the unavailing arguments of angry Brexiters.

At first I was angry with James because he was dismantling the arguments I had been using for just under a year as to why it is a good idea to leave the EU. Slowly but surely I realised that he was using the kind of critical thinking that I should have used when confronted with all the reasons to leave.

His programme became a regular part of my life after that working-holiday. Every Monday to Friday between the hours of 10am and 1pm I tuned in to find out the latest on the Brexit debate. My political education had begun. It became apparent that I was mislead, misinformed, played, cheated and I was angry about it.

The moment came when I was shouting at the radio. Not at James but at the caller who kept trying to dodge James' question. I was infuriated that this faceless caller had the stupidity to call a radio journalist like James without any previous thought about what he was going on air to say and how ridiculous it sounded.

Over the next two years I came to realise that during the 2016 Referendum no one had mentioned in detail:

- The Good Friday Agreement - The agreement between the Island of Ireland and Northern Ireland
- Article 7 - The European legislation that imposes fair rules on how EU members can settle in other countries and by what conditions they can be sent back
- The Medicine Trade - How some life-saving medicines could be un-available to us in the UK
- The need for custom checks in Ireland and Dover
- Brits abroad potentially losing their pensions
- Reports of losing access to an EU-wide crime database
- The possible collapse of the farming industry if we have a no-deal, which the Farmers Union were publicly concerned about
- The contest of workers rights
- The possible increase of mobile roaming fees
- The statuses of Brits living in EU territories and EU members living here in the UK

The list goes on. I also got an education on what the ECJ (European Court of Justice) was and how it played a part in the EU. I discovered that stories such as the EU putting trade standards on how bendy bananas had to be was complete nonsense. I got an education on how the Leave campaign was run, who was running it and how it was funded.

Most importantly, I was receiving the education I should have got when at school. Why isn't politics taught at school? I find it amazing now, that a country/government doesn't want the electorate as a whole educated on how British politics works and moreover, how the European Union works. The next generation of voters, unable to make informed decisions on who leads them.

The Leave campaign has very little to hold on to now. Most of the time someone will shout "it's the will of the people!" Well, I voted for this Brexit rubbish but what is happening right now is not reflective of why I voted to leave. "17.4 Million people have spoken!" I am one of the 17.4 Million and I have not finished speaking.

By this point I had made my mind up. I had made a big mistake and unknowingly to James O'Brien, I was about to take my first steps in political campaigning which was set to change my life forever.

**Enter RemainerNow**

First I asked myself how to get my new political views seen/heard? Easy; most politicians are on twitter. Although I had a twitter account since 2013, I never got the hang of it so I logged back in to start following people from all sorts of political backgrounds and continue my political education. At first I was just watching and taking notes. I Followed @femi_sorry who at the time, was the only person I could relate to.

It wasn't long before RemainerNow found me. I was having some sort of an argument on twitter and RemainerNow retweeted my response. (Above) In no time at all I was putting my name down for every opportunity going. In only two months I had done two videos explaining why I changed my mind for PeoplesVote and RemainerNow social media, I had written an article for PMP (Politics Means Politics) Magazine, written an article for the Metro and been apart of a group invited to Parliament to speak to cross party MP's.

**Plymouth Lib Dems** ◈ @PlymouthLibDems · Nov 2, 2019

An added bonus for local members today was a talk from @ChrisOram1990, spokesperson for the @remainernow campaign who is working hard sharing the #remainernow stories. Thank you so much for joining us, Chris

#itsoktochangeyourmind to #StopBrexit ◈ ■

Sima Davarian ◈ and Sarah Martin Lib Dem ◈

◯          ↻ 4                    ♥ 12                    ↥

It didn't stop there either. The team at RemainerNow had been to Parliament several times and taken part in Peoples Vote rallies up and down the country. I have been part of the team at the Liberal Democrat party conference in September 2019 where I gave speeches at two events, made videos for our social media, got involved with fellow LibDems and voted on party policy.

## Whats next for me?

Great question. I am a Labour leaver turned Liberal Democrat Remainer and I have every intention of making our country aware and comfortable with the idea of changing your opinion of political allegiances.

I have sent my application to become a candidate for the Liberal Democrats and will hopefully run to be a Member of Parliament one day. God willing, the country will soon be ready for liberal values in Westminster.

**Why is RemainerNow still so important?**

"If a democracy cannot change its mind, it ceases to be a democracy" - David Davis MP

We will continue to be a place for people who have changed their minds to come and share their stories. We voted in 2016 for a direction but we were never consulted about the destination. This was always the premise of the second referendum. Of course, leavers from all persuasions don't like this argument but their failure to employ a sensible rebuttal speaks volumes. One of the very many lessons I have learnt since 2016 is that there is a major difference between the words 'argument' and 'debate'. Hardline Brexiteers have nothing to debate a second referendum, therefore they will just regurgitate meaningless soundbites which, when looked at under a microscope, resembles an argument of a child and not a debate between serious political thinkers.

**Why you bought this book**

What you're about to read are the individual stories from people who would now call themselves RemainerNows. Some have been written exclusively for this book. Others have been pulled off our website and other articles (permissions granted) to allow you to see how the debate has changed and how deep our disappointment goes. Some have been written more recently, others have been with us from the beginning.

Turn the page with an open mind, a forgiving heart and with our motto firmly in your brain:

'It's ok to change your mind'

## PART TWO
### RemainerNow Stories

### Emma - Southend on Sea, Essex
### #The5million reasons I changed my mind

My name is Emma and I am from Essex. I am the mother of 2 beautiful boys who happen to have low functioning autism and other severe learning disabilities. During the referendum, I was very scared and unsure how to vote.

Services in my hometown have been cutback and under the assurance of Mr Hannan and others that we would be staying in the Single Market at least, the big red bus pledge of £350 million for our frontline services, I was swayed to voting leave. I always have wanted a deep and good relationship with the EU so to hear Mr Farage the day after the referendum say on Good Morning Britain that the pledge was a "mistake" by Vote Leave, I felt stunned, sick and shocked.

As my vote to leave was swayed by a 'mistake,' what else would be deemed to be a mistake?

I tried to see how things would go and over the month's that followed felt horrified to see the nasty way in which the EU and EU Citizens were being treated in the UK. The graffiti saying "EU rats go home" was horrendous and it has had an impact on friends and people in my community, no one voted for that. No one deserves that! This is our home equally and together. It was promised the rights of EU Citizens in the UK and British In Europe would be guaranteed! My rights are theirs and I refused then and still do to have anyone put in limbo.

There is no difference between us and I reject this forced division. How can anyone be expected to see how things go whilst being treated so poorly after making our land a home? I think of families like mine. How can a child or adult who is vulnerable who happens to be an EU citizen be told to leave and go to a place they do not know or communicate? Everyone deserves a loving home and to be treated with respect and dignity and by heaven, that is not a hard thing to guarantee. We are one people.

During this time, I was able to read the books 'In Limbo' and 'In Limbo Too' – amazing brave  collection of personal stories from EU Citizens in the UK, British In Europe and more by Elena Remegi. I was crushed and

23

moved by their experiences and courage. I wanted to act too but was unsure how to even start.

This division was not in my name or in the name of the many leave voters I know. This was when I started to become more vocal and came across Hugh and RemainerNow. I wasn't alone in feeling used and was able to not only meet people like me but could find a way to ensure it was known that this was not what I voted for.

RemainerNow helped me go to parliament to meet with MPs and Peers, helped be able to meet Steve Bray and all the amazing people of SODEM Action. I have been able to meet amazing grassroots groups like In Limbo Brexit, The 3 Million, British in Europe, Final Say For All, Jane Stevenson of The Yellow Rose initiative, EU Citizens Champion and so many more.

I have never felt more proud of the people in my country and continent because I see their love, passion, peacefulness, compassion and strength every day.

I was nervous about coming out as a RemainerNow but I don't regret it. Everyone has been amazingly supportive and even when I am challenged, I get it. I have had no bad experiences and as RemainerNow Often say, it is always okay to change your mind. It is so true.

So much is still unknown and sadly everyone is still in a horrible situation but we all can do something about it. I go to Westminster to protest for Equal citizen Rights when I can between school runs and between work, I have participated in marches three times and have spoken publicly both locally and in conventions.

You do not have to do big things to make a difference. So many EU Citizens in the UK and British In Europe are sadly experiencing the most uncomfortable situation. Many I love have told me that the conversation they have with those they know can hurt by comments made like "Don't worry, you will be okay because you are the right sort of immigrant" or "when will you go back?". It is so painful yet those I know never say anything because they don't want to hurt anyone, that is how amazing so many are. They take so much pain but don't want to risk anyone feeling that way back.

Please, let's protect our people. We are still one people. Being mindful of each other and showing that we care can make such an amazing difference. For me, I don't want anyone suffering like this simply because I fell for "mistake" . I want to own my "mistake" and make sure everyone is guaranteed their rights whatever happens and check to see if we all really do still want this.

We can all do so much. Just know it is always okay to change your mind and it is easy to be mindful of what we say to those we love, no matter where we are or who we are.

### Alan - Taunton Devon

There are few amongst the general population who can legitimately claim that politics is their area of expertise. It's certainly a claim I cannot make. I don't have all the answers and I freely admit there are contradictions in my thinking I still need to iron out but this is exactly the reason why we elect representatives to parliament and also why we have a free press. We trust our politicians to make decisions on our behalf and we trust our journalists to hold them to account so with that in mind, it does perhaps call into question why such a momentous decision was distilled into an overly simplistic binary choice and placed in the hands of the electorate in the first place.

I am little more than a retail customer assistant doing his utmost to make good decisions based on the information I have to hand and in 2016, when presented with the choice, I chose to leave. In the three years that followed it has become startlingly clear that this decision was flawed.

Firstly, I think it's important for each of us to understand and acknowledge that there were legitimate reasons for voting either way. I don't naturally align with the likes of Boris Johnson and Nigel Farage however, in 2016, I found myself agreeing with the principle that parliament should be sovereign. I believe in democracy, independence and self determination and if a community wishes to govern itself it should be free to do so. I will always view this as a legitimate reason in favour of leaving any union but I have since learned that this is an incredibly narrow and simplistic way of viewing our relationship and role within the EU with our perceived lack of control greatly exaggerated by some.

Unlike hardcore Brexit advocates, I accepted that there were many excellent reasons for voting remain and I didn't judge anyone for doing so. As a peace project, the European Union has been nothing other than a complete success and it is steadfast in protecting the rights of its millions of citizens.

I maintain that my vote to leave was not about sticking two fingers up to Europe; it was not about ending freedom of movement nor was it about sending foreigners "back home" and it certainly wasn't about leaving the single market. It was what I considered to be a respectful "no thank you" to further political and judicial integration within the European Union. It was a way for me to express my mistrust of the type of democracy the EU operates and that, in principle, the UK should always have a final say on anything and everything relating to our interests.

26

I looked at the arrangements of Norway and Switzerland and decided that, on balance, it would be something more suited to the UK than membership. Indeed, it was one of many options repeatedly discussed by many of those prominent in the Leave campaign when the very idea of "no-deal" was dismissed by everyone. As many of them said at the time, it would be the easiest negotiation in history because Britain held all the cards.

Having voted both Labour and Green in the past, on this issue I felt I aligned with the government and the Conservatives. As the party that has always claimed to champion entrepreneurial spirit and business as well as it's repeated boasts of having an excellent track record in maintaining and managing a strong economy, I put my trust in them as the people best placed to negotiate the only type of Brexit that made sense to me. I was expecting our negotiations to be hard but fair and conducted with a spirit of mutual respect, compromise and co-operation so that we could still enjoy a prosperous relationship with our European friends, neighbours and allies whilst regaining some areas of control I believed we had given up to Brussels.

Clearly, I was wrong. It didn't happen the way I expected and instead we have been led into a national crisis of epic proportions. Unfortunately, I did not have the foresight to anticipate what was going to happen as a result of my decision and in hindsight I realise I fixated too much on principle instead of pragmatism. I should have voted to remain so that we could work to reform what we did not like.

At this point in August 2019 with businesses set to leave the country, repeated warnings from industry experts about the critical disruption of food and medical supplies into the country, a gridlocked parliament, a Conservative party now under the thumb of hard right ERG (European Research Group led by Jacob Rees-Mogg) members and a government with a massive majority of one led by, of all people, Boris Johnson, I cannot see how Brexit will be anything other than a failure and I am not so entrenched or tribal in my views that I refuse to face up to and apologise for my role in this. Regardless of the questionable conduct of the Leave campaign and many areas of the press that allowed their lies to go unchallenged we are each responsible for the choices that we make and I should have been more thorough in my research prior to voting.

In 2016 we "held all the cards" in 2019 we can make a no-deal Brexit work because "we survived two world wars" seventy years ago. This is madness.

Like many up and down the country on both sides of this issue I have been left angry, appalled and frustrated by a party more concerned with their own prosperity and their own survival than that of the country they were elected to lead. I am disgusted with those who set this chain of events in motion and then bailed on Brexit the minute the result came through choosing instead to spend three years heckling from the sidelines offering absolutely nothing. We had a Prime Minister in Theresa May who obliterated her majority in an election she should never have called, who was enthralled by the ERG and the DUP and who had no willingness or intention to listen and compromise and now the likes of Johnson, Gove, Raab and Farage have returned to finish what they started by presenting the worst of what they promised as the best.

To be clear: I categorically did not vote for no deal and WTO (World Trade Organisation) terms overnight. I haven't yet heard a logical, coherent plan for this scenario except hope and pray and I believe it would be catastrophic if it occurred. This view is not uncommon among many regretful leave voters. As a result my current position is this: if you are going to do something, you do it right or you do not do it at all. We should not leave the EU in this manner which is why I continue to support the revocation of Article 50 subject to a public vote.

I consider myself to be an honest and forthright person and when I'm proven wrong I'm obliged to hold my hands up and admit it. It shouldn't be considered a brave thing to do, it should simply be the norm. I signed the Revoke Article 50 petition before it reached a million signatures and engaged with a tweet from Brian Cox which is where I found many decent, respectful remain voters who wanted to listen to what I had to say, understand my reasoning and who supported my change of heart. This is how I came to be involved with RemainerNow.

I don't know if remaining in the EU is a possibility. I don't know if there's time left to persuade enough Leave voters to change their minds and make their voices heard and if they did, I don't know if the establishment would even listen but regardless of what does happen, in the aftermath of Brexit, groups like RemainerNow will be critical in continuing to bridge that divide by encouraging respectful discourse between both sides and welcoming those who've looked again at the facts and reached a different conclusion.

**Kate Westerham, Kent**

I voted Leave and I thought at the time that I was helping my country. I now realise that my vote has harmed it and for that I am profoundly sorry.

I thought that I was helping the NHS. I believed the lie on the bus.
I thought that I was helping the British farmers and fisherman.
I thought that the EU had too much say on how we ran our country.

As soon as the result was announced I began to realise that maybe I had made a mistake. I heard lots of racist abuse from Leavers and I was horrified. Also the fact that Johnson backed away from the leaders contest as if he was surprised that leave had won and didn't know what to do next. I finally changed my mind when I saw that the Irish Border problem would be very difficult if not impossible to solve and that to leave, we would be turning our backs on Ireland. This would not help my country, this would split the UK. I started to verify reports from news papers and social media and found many lies to the leave argument.

The NHS relies heavily on the skills of an EU and immigrant workforce. Yes, we pay the EU a lot of money but we get quite a lot of it back. A lot of money from the EU has gone to the north of England and Wales. Looking into this I found that a £3000 grant was paid to a business only 10 mins walk away from me by the EU. None of this came to my notice in the leave campaign. I am worried that we will be so desperate for a trade deal with the US that we will be held over a barrel and that we will end up selling off our NHS to the US. Not project fear, Johnson and many members of the cabinet have stated that they want to privatise the NHS. I believe at least 70 MPs have interests in private medicine. Why is Trump so eager for Brexit? He has always said US first, there is no special relationship. US pharmaceutical companies cannot wait to get into the UK. I did not vote for this.

As for farming, yes we do appear to get a bad deal with the CAP but our politicians haven't exactly stood up for our farmers within the EU. Would that change if we came out of the EU? I'm not convinced, our farmers live in the countryside far away from Westminster. Many famers could go out of business because they will lose their subsidies plus they rely heavily on EU nationals for farm labour. I cannot see British people working the fields, it is hard work. I am worried that we would have to trade with the US and China for our food. Their animal welfare is not as high as ours. I understand that we will have to lower our standards to enable us to import from these countries. I trust the EU regulations for our food and animal welfare. I do not want to buy from China or the USA.

There is a lot of stuff out there that says that the EU isn't accountable to us. I believe that that it is partly our fault. We generally don't really take much notice when MEPs come up for election. I feel unhappy that we are about to place all the power into Westminster. I attended a protest in a town near me to try and prevent the proroguing of parliament. We stood outside our local conservative office and they just looked out of the window and laughed. Couldn't even be bothered to speak to us. We were held in contempt. The EU isn't perfect but I would rather be part of the 27 than little England on it's own trying to negotiate a trade deal or trying to protect itself from Russia. I did not vote for this.

This attitude of "just get Brexit done" really annoys me. If we leave the EU, government and the civil service etc will be tied up for years negotiating new trade deals and amending or making new laws. In the meantime general running of the country will be hindered by this process. The only way that we can get on with our lives is to stay in the EU. Let parliament govern and let the EU take care of negotiating trade deals.

We need free movement of people for the future of the NHS and in fact our everyday lives rely on free movement and immigration. I do not want these essential people to feel unwanted and under valued. I did not vote for that. I thought that I was protecting the UK when in fact Scotland and Wales are now looking for independence. We are safer within the EU for our security, food regulations, NHS, jobs and workers rights.

The UK will always come first for me but I now feel that I am a European and I am very proud of this and I do not want to lose it.

### Mikey - Rochester, Kent

#### Why I voted leave.

I voted leave in 2016, one of the biggest motivating factors for me was lack of connection with the EU, Fact is, all the family passports had run out at the end of 2008, and due to the socioeconomics of the UK, I was unable to afford new passports, there was always something else to buy, repair or re-place, the passports had in my view become a luxury, not a necessity.

So When the EU referendum happened in 2016, it had been 8 years since we last visited the EU, by that time the connection I had with the EU had gone, to me it had become some place over there, hardly relevant anymore, fact is I was struggling financially, despite the economy apparently going up, I wasn't seeing it, costs had gone up, but not the wages, & it wasn't just that, passports aside, you had the travel costs too, during the school holidays the costs are exploitive.

So when the EU referendum came in 2016, I listened and watched both sides, but in all honesty StrongerIn and the other 'Remain' campaigns didn't do it for me, their campaigns were horrifically bad, it was mostly doom & gloom. I didn't see or hear much positive messages from 'Remain,' there was no emotive draw to them at all, no connection as such. When they did eventually get round to the positives, like freedom of movement being the only one they really mentioned, well I couldn't afford passports anyway, so to my family and me, it wasn't exactly a big loss.

The 'leave' side was offering things 'remain' wasn't, or couldn't I suppose. A chance for change, the chance for a better future, a break from the Status Quo. Aside from the Bile, They offered something else: hope. Something the Remain campaign never did.

#### Why I changed my mind.

To be honest, I started having doubts soon after the EU referendum, though they were not solid doubts as such, more fleeting, occasional doubts, easily dismissed etc.

That all started to change round about August 2016, when I came across a gentlemen on Twitter called Mike, we naturally started chatting about Brexit, why I voted the way I did and why he voted the way he did.

Over a period of a few months, whilst we were chatting, Mike started to introduce new concepts, new ways of understanding how and why I voted the way I did. He basically opened doors for me that I never thought about, or considered possible, so much so that I finally took the risk and bought all the family passports. By the time April 2017 (First trip to Paris and the first time out of the country in nine years) had come, I had pretty much turned from a "Leave" position to a "Remain" position.

Since then, I have been to Paris, Rome, Amsterdam, Brugge, The Hague, Rotterdam, Boulougne and many more places inside the EU. For the first time in a long time I understood a little about what freedom of movement is about (albeit from a travel point of view). Speaking to citizens of the EU-27 in EU counties about what the EU is like. What it does, what it is, and after seeing and understanding what the UK is like from a European perspective, I'm ashamed in part to be British. After witnessing what has happened in the UK last three plus years, it's actually pushed me further on from just 'Remaining,' I actually believe in closer integration now, Schengen, The Euro, an EU Army and everything right up to federalisation. What we need is more equality, same laws, same currency, same government.

Having now experienced some of the basic fundamental rights and privileges of EU citizenship, I don't want to lose them, I don't want my family to lose them. The problems the UK was never caused by the European Union, the problems were caused by the laziness, ineptitude, selfishness of our elected politicians, who over the last 3-4 decades preferred to blame the EU for their own failures and their own over-reliance on short-term gimmick solutions that created long-term problems.

The UK as a whole, needs to reject British exceptionalism, it needs to start embracing the EU, not fearing it, we (The UK as a whole) needs to stop being so inward looking.

Since then, I have come into contact with two specific groups: Remainer-Now & FinalSayForAll. Connecting with RemainerNow has helped me quite a lot. It has introduced me to other people who have changed their minds and made me realise that I'm not as alone as perhaps I once thought. Connecting with FinalSayForAll has helped me connect with the 5Million, helped me understand their perspectives and consequences of any Brexit.

Now personally, I'm even in favour of just revoking Article 50 but if we must have a Peoples Vote, then it must include the 5 million. Those who couldn't vote last time, if not the 5 million, then at very least it should include the EU Citizens who have made their lives here. They and the Brits in the EU have as much right to vote as I do. If anything it's more important that they vote than I do, they have much more at stake than me.

### Leon - Doncaster, South Yorkshire

In the EU Referendum in 2016 I voted to leave the European Union. At the time I was proud to support our efforts to leave the EU and bring about change to our politics, a change that would be to the betterment of all people across the United Kingdom. How wrong was I?

I admit that in the run up to the referendum I wasn't totally sure which way to vote. Being from Doncaster, I shared the frustration of many people in my area that Westminster simply does not listen. For decades, my area has not improved and it hasn't mattered which party has been in power. Westminster seemed a million miles away and our concerns simply weren't being heard. Imagine how far away Brussels appeared.

Eventually I came to the conclusion that the best way forward for the UK was to leave the EU, a protectionist, antidemocratic stagnant club with no regard for the concerns of the citizens in its member states, or so I thought. Leaving the EU would be a wake up call to our political establishment. It would remind them that they cannot simply ignore people who don't live in marginal constituencies. It should be noted that I didn't think for a second that the Leave Campaign would actually win. I believed that the bleak statements from the Remain Campaign would win the day, and that fear would triumph over hope.

On the morning of the 27th June 2016, I turned on the news and I was stunned. In my view, the public had seen through the misplaced pessimism of the Remain Campaign and demanded change. No longer would the people's voice be dismissed. I was delighted and full of hope.

I was backing Brexit well into 2018, but I began having concerns. When the details of Theresa May's Brexit deal were made public, I felt deflated. This wasn't a positive deal I felt I could support. By this point, many prominent Leave campaigners had already been talking up the possibility of leaving without a deal. Even the Prime Minister at the time, Theresa May, had uttered those ridiculous words: "no deal is better than a bad deal".

I knew then that leaving without a deal was not something I had voted for. I wanted a close relationship with the EU post-Brexit and I wanted an orderly exit, not a chaotic crash. Despite this setback, I continued supporting Brexit and hoping that a positive deal could be reached that would be to the benefit of both the UK and the EU. This wasn't to be the case though. No positivity came about. And yet I continued on stubbornly, talking up what I saw as the benefits of Brexit.

In December 2018, I read the Doncaster Free Press and saw that the Best for Doncaster group, a pro-EU campaign group based in Doncaster, would be holding a street stall in the town centre. I knew that this group was calling for a People's Vote and I knew that I disagreed with that position, so I decided I would go along and tell them as such. I walked up to the street stall and politely introduced myself.

> *"Hello, my name's Leon, good to see people still passionate about this but don't you think it's wrong to call for another vote before the first one has even been implemented?" The campaigner smiled and replied "I take it you voted to leave the EU? Out of interest, do you support the deal that Theresa May has brought back?"*

(While asking this I was being handed a sticker to put on their mood board to show whether I voted leave and whether I backed a People's Vote or not)

> *I confirmed that I did not support the deal. She asked me if I supported no deal. I said that I did not support a no deal. It might seem a bit dim of me, but she then asked me the question that really made me think. "You don't support the deal that the Government has brought back and you don't support leaving without a deal. These are the only two options being presented by the Government. Don't you think you should have a say on that?"*

It's an obvious question with an obvious answer, but I hadn't previously been asked it so never really gave it any thought previously. But it was such a good question because she was right and I couldn't argue against it. I talked to her about why I didn't support either of the options presented by the Government and how unhappy I would be if either of those options happened, and that's when I realised. Why back this thing I clearly don't support anymore and why deny myself the opportunity to send that message to the Government? I backed Brexit partly because I felt the public was being ignored by Westminster. Now I was backing Brexit despite the fact the public was being ignored by Westminster. I now knew where to put my sticker. "Do you know what? You're right. We should remain." The campaigner was stunned and hurriedly got the attention of the Chair of Best for Doncaster to let her know they'd found a convert. I ended up doing a video for the group to go on social media explaining my change of mind and that's when I discovered RemainerNow.

Since then I have been speaking a lot about my change of mind. I've written in my local paper, I wrote a piece of The Independent and spoke at the Put it to the People Rally in Leeds in June 2019 and spoke at the Leeds for Europe Rally in September 2019. The response from original Remainers has been warm and welcoming, something I didn't expect.

What has really struck me though all this, is the division in our country. To say these divisions were brought about by Brexit is too simplistic. These divisions have been present for years but have now been exposed. Brexit will not solve the problems we have though. Governments of all stripes have let down our nation but we have been blaming the wrong people. We have to demand better from our Governments, not outsource blame to the EU.

If anything, Brexit will deepen the divisions we see in society, especially if we follow through with a disastrous no deal Brexit. The Government's own impact assessments have stated that the worst off in society will be hardest hit. This cannot be accepted. We cannot accept a scenario where we are driven off a cliff following a policy that has no democratic mandate.

This is now more than just about whether leaving the EU is the right thing to do. This is now a question about our democracy. Does a brief snapshot of public opinion constitute democracy, or do we accept that opinions can change? The answer to this question will change how we view democracy and how we do politics for generations. We must get this right.

### Lisa - Wakefield, West Yorkshire

I'll start by saying my name is Lisa, I'm from Wakefield West Yorkshire, I've been married for 33 years. I have three adult sons and one grandson, and I'm a #RemainerNow. I voted leave in the 2016 referendum because, I wanted more money for the NHS.

I think the reason for this was because, without going into too much detail, in September 2011 my husband had a life changing accident where he broke his neck, and then 11 months later, I lost my mum to bowel cancer. On both of these occasions the NHS were absolutely amazing. But, even back then the cuts to the NHS were having an effect. After my husbands accident, he used to, and still does go on pain forums where he speaks to other people in the same situation as him. He speaks to a lot of people from the USA, and they constantly tell him how they have had to sell their houses once their insurance runs out, to be able to afford their pain relief. Also I was so shocked and horrified when he told me some have committed suicide because they didn't want to be a burden financially on their families, because they couldn't afford their pain relief anymore. So hearing these stories made me so much more appreciative of our NHS. I remember seeing on social media articles about immigrants using the NHS without paying into the system getting houses by jumping the queue on housing waiting lists, whilst going straight onto benefits.

Wow, as I'm writing this I feel so ashamed of myself for falling for all the, what I'd call now, right wing propaganda. I was really angry, so when the leave campaign started I think I was ready to believe what they told us, to me it all made sense.

I thought there was too much pressure on the NHS, housing and schools, because of immigration. I am not against immigration I just thought at that time, we should have more control on who and how many people were coming here from the EU. So leaving the EU would mean less people using the NHS and less children in schools. Less pressure generally on our services.

So I think I blamed the EU for all the problems the country was having at that time, where instead, when I look back now, I should have blamed our own government and their policies that they had put into place.

Remember when the leave campaign said £350 million a week for the NHS? Yes, I know, I believed what was on the side of that bloody big red bus. OMG how gullible was I? Christ knows the NHS needed it!

I remember the leave campaign saying how we'd be able to negotiate really quick and easy future trade agreements with the EU at the same time as negotiating the withdrawal agreement, after all they need us more than we need them! They basically said that we could have all the benefits without having to pay millions of pounds each week.

On the night of the results I sat with my middle son who voted remain to watch the results together. Even after seeing how upset he was that leave "won", I still thought I'd done the right thing by voting leave. The following February in 2017 I found out I had breast cancer and had to have a lumpectomy and radiotherapy. Again the NHS were absolutely amazing, and I was still thinking once we're out of the EU there'll be more money for the NHS.

So fast forward two years after the vote and I started to realise things weren't going the way we were told by the leave campaign. David Davis after all his bravado of how easy these negotiations were going to be, had backed down on negotiating the future trade agreements alongside the withdrawal agreement. The EU would not negotiate the future trade agreements until our divorce agreement was signed. Then it seemed to all unravel, once the withdrawal agreement was agreed, the then Prime Minister tried to get it through parliament, & failed, mainly because of the backstop. Who'd ever heard of the backstop, before that vote? I hadn't.

I was realising more and more that things weren't anything like we'd been told. Migrants coming here could be deported to their home country, if they hadn't found a job within a limited time, but our government just didn't use that option. Also most migrants that had come here were working and contributing to the pot. The real problem was that our government weren't investing in our schools, our NHS or building new housing. I found out that the leave campaign had broke electoral law. I felt so foolish and ashamed that I'd voted for something that actually wasn't achievable.

So now I feel everything I voted for was a lie, I feel like my vote was stolen from me. I hate that I fell for all the lies. I feel now I have to fight to get my vote back so I can vote on the true information I have now. I feel that I have put the NHS at more risk than it was before the referendum, because the USA could use it, by demanding access to it, amongst other things, to get a trade deal with them, how ironic is that? I feel so sick that my vote to leave could've helped the path to privatise our beloved NHS.

I also can't accept that there are no consequences for breaking electoral law by the leave campaign, other than, to give them a comparatively measly fine. They should not be allowed to effectively buy the result they want. There are so many things being revealed now that, are so shocking. Our PM has employed as special advisor to the government, Dominic Cummings who was Director of the official leave campaign and who was found in contempt of parliament, for refusing to go in front of the parliamentary select committee, to answer questions about fake news during the leave campaign. Also our government is now heading towards leaving the EU without a deal. I really and truly believe the public should be able to vote on this again with an option to remain, and I will definitely vote to remain, if I'm given that chance.

### James - Halifax, West Yorkshire

I voted leave in 2016 because I believed that my generation deserved a vote on our future with Europe. I grew up in Yorkshire, my father was a local conservative councillor and even ran for the referendum party in 1997. So I got told when things went wrong it was Europe's fault. I believed the EU was run by unelected bureaucrats, which I thought was rather unfair.

When we got discover we were having a referendum, I was happy. I even got involved with a pro Brexit business group in the Yorkshire region. I remember when I was attending a business conference in Leeds in May before the vote, Nigel Farage was speaking on the panel and he came across rather well. The only countenance for remain was a student manning a stand asking if I wanted a sticker.

I was also advised that we would remain in the Customs Union and Single Market, and if that was to become a fact, then there would be another vote on that. If you looked at all the opinion polls, remain was always ahead, so I thought what the heck, it can be a protest vote against Cameron and Austerity, not for a moment thinking leave would win. The vote was the wrong question at the right time.

I changed my mind quite soon after the vote. I hadn't taken into account the negative effect it was to have on my family. My wife is from Germany, and when we would out leave had won, I felt sick. What had I done? The promises of protected status for EU residents quickly evaporated along with all the other promises for the NHS, staying in the single market etc.

I hadn't even considered the possibility of us removing our own rights to work, live and travel across the whole of Europe. Oh is only that was on a side of a bus. As I watched to my horror all leave campaign pledges got twisted by the hard right Brexiteers and I'm ashamed to have being fooled by all the lies. What is worse is that the Government took a hard Brexit approach, which they didn't even change when they lost their majority in the 2017 election.

I felt I could no longer stay on the sidelines and I had to take a pro-active approach to change the current path. I was approached by Andy from RemainerNow, via twitter if I wanted to speak at a People's Vote Rally outside the Conservative party conference in Birmingham. I was a bag of nerves, but thankfully the crowds were kind and I had many thanks for speaking out. At the time, the government had refused to believe that anyone had changed their minds. It winds me up when the Brexiteers bring up the 17.4million figure. That is no longer accurate. I've gone onto having two visits to the Houses of Parliament with RemainerNow, People's Vote rally in Leeds and Manchester, videos for Peoples Vote and Led by Donkeys and now as I write this, I'm on my way to Brussels to meet MEP's on the 17th October 2019. I hope and pray we don't leave on 31st October this year, and we get to have another say and put a stop to the madness that has become Brexit.

### Carol - Brighton, Sussex

Less than 1.3M out of a country of 66M decided the future of the United
Kingdom. A country that had been battered by years of austerity, years of
resentment towards David Cameron's government. Also, at that time, the
spectre of a Trump presidency was no more than a joke.

Some people believed the Leave campaign's lies such as the NHS millions,
the millions of Turks heading to the UK, some believed Britain would get
an easy trade deal with the EU. Others, like me, considered it an opportunity
to make a protest vote against the EU's proposed T-TIP deal, which, according to my local branch of Unison, would threaten workers rights, sell off the
NHS and wreck our environmental protection. Sound familiar?

I'll be frank, at the time of the referendum I had a lot of personal issues. My
mum had passed away in December 2015, after over six years of suffering
Alzheimers/vascular dementia. If anyone has any personal experience of
this disease, they will understand how it drains the sufferer's family too. I
was at rock-bottom emotionally, I had so much to sort out whilst continuing
to work in a stressful job. My mind was not up to the task of finding out the
truth behind Brexit, or the lies about the EU. To say I regret voting Leave is
an understatement.

Every single day, since 23 June 2016 I have felt profound guilt, and utter
despair with the Brexit debacle. If I had known back then, what I know
now, there would be no way I'd even contemplate voting Leave. Stupidly, I
thought I was safe in making a protest vote, because I believed the polls.
The pollsters predicted a safe Remain win, and to be fair, before my head hit
the pillow that was the prediction. Imagine how I felt the next day when I
woke to see Farage gloating on breakfast TV. I felt numb, I felt sick and I
felt extreme anger at my stupidity. A mere majority of 1,269,501 gave Farage reason to gloat and make a lot of dosh on the collapse of Sterling I suspect.

Of course now, thanks to Twitter and the marvellous people who have done
a lot of digging, I'm now aware of the truth. Brexit is nothing to do with
leaving the EU without a deal because of the 'will of the people,' but it is
everything to do with the 'will of the super-rich.' To be clear, the race to
leave the EU by the 31st October 2019, is everything to do with the Brex-
Con donors, Boris's backers, US lobbyists & Putin backed advisors.

If there is one positive I can take from this whole ghastly experience, is the camaraderie of the anti-Brexit movement. Initially, we were quite understandably hounded by Remainers, now we are generally welcomed. My confidence has massively increased too.

If someone had told me back in 2015, I would be assertive enough to go on my own to my first mass march on 23 June 2018, speak with cross-party MPs in the House of Commons, have the nerve to confront Michael Gove about the claim that he'd "never met anyone who's changed their minds," (I forced him into speaking to the RN delegation) Addressing thousands on stage at a rally in Parliament Square, and also, in October 2019, travelling to Brussels as part of a RemainerNow delegation for a round-table discussion with MEPs. Having done all of this, and so much more, I would have laughed them out of the room.

I have met some fabulous people on the rocky road of Brexit, many of whom I can call friends now. I'll always be grateful to Andy & Victoria who run RemainerNow – without them, I'm not sure where I would be. Big thanks to the SODEM protest in Westminster too, for providing a sanctuary for like-minded people, as well as reminding the media – Remainers will never go away.

From the 1st January 2020 the EU Offshore Tax directive will crack down on these multi-millionaires, oligarchs whose investments are kept far, far away from the HMRC. That sickens me. A No Deal Brexit will not affect the likes of Banks, Rees-Mogg, Crispin Odey, Farage, Boris Johnson and pals. Once the dirty deed is done, I doubt if we'll see their sorry backsides for dust.

This is why every day I feel intense rage, because the tax-evading reason for Brexit is never dealt with in the mainstream media. Therefore, the con continues, but I also hold Remain politicians guilty of withholding this vital information, because each and every time they are interviewed on TV or in the press, this information should continually be referred to when questioned about Brexit.

I'm angry, I'm scared, once again my mental health is deteriorating, my relationships have suffered because, I misguidedly voted Leave. I do not want to exist in post-No Deal Brexit Britain, or rather in a dystopian, authoritarian England (as UK will be finished).

Not all Leave voters were, or are Brexiteers.

## Karen - Great Yarmouth, Norfolk

I didn't have strong feelings about the EU before the referendum was called, and so when it was, I wanted to make sure that I had some idea of our relationship before I made a decision. I did feel uneasy about how such a huge establishment could govern in a way that kept 28 countries happy and secure when it seemed to me that devolution was the way forward.

I wanted to look for some facts about our membership of the EU, the costs and the benefits, so I could decide for myself whether this club was one I wanted to stay in or not. I really struggled, I couldn't seem to find any straightforward, black and white facts regarding our membership.

From every angle all I seemed to find were negatives, that leaving the EU would be terrible (Project Fear) or that the EU itself was awful. Many people seemed to already have their opinions, in fact some questioned why I was even bothering to research as in their view it was obvious that we HAD to Leave/Remain and that was that. I found myself making my decision as I stood in the Polling Station looking at my Ballot Paper.

"Let's give it a go, how bad can it be?"

I stayed up to watch the results, and despite voting Leave, I was shocked when "we" won, I had genuinely thought that Remain would win. That reaction now makes me question just what percentage of my vote had been a protest, my chance to stick two fingers up to the government whether I acknowledged that at the time or not. At least with such a close result, the soft, close, cosy Brexit I'd preferred would now be more likely. Surely....

I can't remember exactly when doubts started. I posted on Facebook the day after the vote, defending my Leave vote, as my timeline had erupted casting all Leave voters as ignorant and racist. I explained why I voted to Leave, and did have some interesting discussions with friends. Those eventually led me to find some of the simple facts, treaties and documents I would have loved to have found before June 23rd 2016.

I remember seeing Steve Bray on the news, constantly, and wanted to know what drove this man to still advocate so strongly that we should stay in the EU. All of this was sowing the seeds of doubt, but I think the death knell into my Leave mentality was when Article 50 was triggered, with no plan in place, no sketch of a plan in place, no nothing in place. The countdown had started and we were all in the dark.

When finally, talk of the deal started, I realised that my idea of Brexit, keeping freedom of movement, keeping all trade agreements and custom agreements but losing the governance of the EU Parliament wasn't even possible. I'd been sold a unicorn, and like an idiot, I'd bought it.

It seemed like forever until a deal finally appeared, and even then it was clear that this "Leave" vote meant 17.4 million things to 17.4 million people, so much so that even the Cabinet didn't agree on the deal. How were we going to find a deal that matched up to the ideals that every individual Leave voter had? What was on the table now certainly bore no resemblance to the future outside of the EU I had pictured prior to marking my X in that box. I was certainly now in the Remain camp, but whilst regretting my vote, still felt that Brexit was likely, and we'd be leaving at the end of March.

Then the deal was voted down. By that time I was feeling strongly enough about Brexit to be watching BBC Parliament, following events far more closely. With the deal obviously being dead in the water, suddenly focus turned to what would happen if there was no deal agreed with the clock ticking every louder in the countdown to March 31st. This terrified me. I had in no way whatsoever voted for this scenario, this was never supposed to happen. That was when I started to get more and more vocal about changing my mind. I voted Leave, but not for this, for a deal, a good deal, the easiest deal ever!

Whenever I'd see the infamous 17.4M thrown about on Twitter, I'd angrily respond, saying that my vote, my voice, was within that number, and in no way was any of this being done in my name. "The Will of the People" extracted the same response. If anyone mentioned either of those on the news, or on BBC Parliament whilst I was watching, I'd be reminding them via Twitter, that my mind had changed, they did not speak for me.

This is how RemainerNow found me, ranting away, not knowing I wasn't alone. It was such a relief to know I wasn't a lone voice hopelessly trying to be heard. I wasn't the only one who had believed lies, who hadn't managed to research every tiny detail of our EU membership, or who (to my utter shame) never gave a thought to Northern Ireland, that leaving would mean a hard EU border.

I felt the weight of this utter shambles on my shoulders, this is partly my fault, I wanted to do SOMETHING to try and mitigate what I'd done. I've written several times to my Conservative MP regarding my change of mind, and my concerns about leaving without a deal. He campaigned to Remain, is now in favour of Leave, but despite me informing him I'd changed my mind too, sees no irony in talking of the Will of the People.

I live in a deprived area, which voted 72% to Leave. I used to have faith that our politicians, whilst I disliked most of them, were ultimately in their position to work in the best interests of their constituents, and their country. Another faith now broken.

As I'm writing this, Parliament has just returned after being unlawfully pro-rogued. The Supreme Court have ruled that the Prime Minister has acted unlawfully. The Yellowhammer documents are being dismissed as Project Fear. The impartiality of the judiciary is being questioned. This is all supposedly being done in my name. How did an advisory vote, that ended in such a close result, lead us here? I feel utterly betrayed, a referendum should never have been called with such an open question.

A plan or outline deal should have been drawn up before the vote, so it was a tangible Leave. That would have eliminated the speculation and downright lies we had to endure from all sides in 2016. As we can't rewind the clock, that's what we need, what we should have had in the first place, an exact description of what Leave means (with an agreed deal with the EU) or to Remain. How else do we sort this out? The General Election in 2017 was supposed to get direction on how to proceed, and that left us in an even bigger mess, so to expect anything other than another hung Parliament is wildly optimistic at best.

This has to be put back to the people.

### Julian - Blandford, Dorset

Just because I'm getting on doesn't mean that I can't look to the future!

I am going to start by telling you a little about myself. I am a 70 year old grandfather who for forty years ran a medium sized manufacturing business. I have a degree in art history and literature, have been a magistrate, am a guide at a National Trust house, been chairman of my local parish council, set up and was the original chairman of the Dorset Association of School Governors.

I joined the Liberal party at the age of 16, was a founder member of the SDP, was chairman of Wimborne Liberal Democrats, resigned when Nick Clegg went into coalition with the Tories and rejoined the party in 2019.

So why do I tell you all of that? There are two reasons: firstly I hope you will conclude that I am a reasonably intelligent human being and secondly I hope that you should be concerned, maybe a little alarmed, that as a liberal minded intelligent human being I should have voted for us the leave the EU back in 2016.

So, let me explain why I took that decision and then what happened in the subsequent couple of years. 2016 was a difficult year for me. My business required greater investment but at 66 years old I was reluctant to risk my financial future so decided I needed to sell up and retire. Getting ready to do this after many years emotionally draining and this coupled with some problems we had had with some EU regulations which materially affected our company made me vulnerable to the emotion and the arguments put forward by the Leave campaigns. Plus who didn't want to give Cameron a kick up the backside?

For a long time I felt that the EU was aimed towards the large financial and industrial conglomerates and was encouraging the formation of Europe-wide mega companies. Running a medium-sized company in that environment made me feel vulnerable and I had several experiences of losing valuable contracts to these large pan-European companies. The EU seemed to offer no protection to smaller businesses

So the clever marketing strategies developed by Cummings, Johnson, Gove, all very familiar strategies that we see employed in government today, seemed to answer some of my business concerns. I was assured by comments such as "The free trade agreement we will have to do should be one of the easiest in human history" so said Liam Fox, or more explicitly "There will continue to be free trade and access to the single market" which was a comment by Boris Johnson.

"We will maintain a free flowing border at Dover" claimed Chris Failing Grayling – well at least he realised that there were lorries queuing to go to France unlike Dominic Raab! "Absolutely no-one is talking about threatening our place in the single market" claimed Daniel Hannan, a Tory MEP.

But it wasn't simply business and trade that I considered when deciding how to vote. I truly wanted to see more investment in the NHS and naïve as it now sounds, was taken in by the promises that the Leave message offered. These promises also included no changes to our security arrangements, scientific partnerships and cultural links plus improvements for our fishing and agricultural industries.

My family and political background had always taught me to be aware of those who have less than me, that we should protect vulnerable members of society and have a safety net for those in desperate straits. The deindustrialisation of this country had led to a terrible north south divide with many people feeling disenfranchised. I believed that this might change if the focus was taken away from the EU and we could concentrate on putting our own house in order.

However I must stress that I did not believe in any restrictions on Freedom of Movement or Immigration and this had no bearing on my voting. I believed that we would maintain close trading links with the EU, the single market, the Customs Union in particular. At no time was the concept of a Hard Brexit or No Deal ever contemplated or indeed ever discussed by the likes of Johnson, Gove, Patel, Grayling etc. - in fact the very opposite.

So why did I change my view?
The day I posted my postal vote I was booked to be away on holiday on Referendum Day. I really was not sure when I voted if I had done the right thing and nor did I really think Leave would win. I actually felt that I was betraying all those things that I had fought for many years but the Remain campaign had been so weak, Cameron and Osborne so smug and confident, Leave had been so clever that I told myself I had done the right thing personally. At three o'clock on the morning of the result I crept down to the living room of my sister and brother in laws house in Portugal, turned on my tablet and like most of you was surprised and alarmed that Leave had

won. So much for giving Cameron a kick up the backside. At that moment I knew I was wrong.

It soon became clear that there were a number of facts that the Leave campaign had stated were actually not true, most especially the money available for the NHS and the status of the Irish border (which Teresa Villiers stated was "no less likely to be less open after Brexit than it is today" ).

The emergence of the ERG and the Brexit Party demanding a No-Deal Brexit is clearly horrifying. This is not simply "regaining our sovereignty" but divorcing ourselves from the international community in an act of extraordinary self-sacrifice. The people most at risk are the most vulnerable in our society.

Now as a father and grandparent I fear for the future for my family. To take away the opportunities afforded by membership of the EU to future generations is a penalty of which my generation should be ashamed. To make up for the mistake I had made back in June 2016 I determined to join the Remainers who wanted to have a Peoples Vote to determine what the result would be if the lies, on both sides, were discounted and when we knew exactly what the arrangements would be in the Withdrawal Agreement.

I have written many times to my MP Simon Hoare, a Remainer who changed to support May's failed Withdrawal Agreement and is now supporting Johnson. I tweet regularly about Remaining and my extended family and I have marched in London on four occasions. My one year old grandson had a large poster on his pram last time saying "My grandson's first words were Bollocks to Brexit!" I have spoken at a #remainernow event at the Lib Dem conference with Chukka Omana and various MEP's and at Lord Adonis' Anti Brexit Tour.

I ask all parents and grandparents who voted Leave and now have doubts to join me and all those of us proud to support #remainernow to campaign to remain. I believe that we owe this to our children, to their children and to all the future generations of this once wonderful country.

### Ben - Swindon, Wiltshire

When I was a little boy, my family would blame immigrants for many things wrong in this country. I would hear things like " there are too many of them," "there isn't enough space in this country," "British people should get homes and healthcare before them, they just come here for our benefits" and many more comments with this theme. Children are impressionable and are a product of their environment and I was no exception. I would go to primary and secondary school and repeat many of these statements due to the conditioning I had received.

On the subject of the EU itself, I never really took a strong interest. Again, I was fed with stories in passing about the bendy bananas and all manner of myths emanating from the tabloids. Due to my lack of interest, I never took the time to seek the truth and as such my view of the EU was coloured. This colouring led me to engage in confirmation bias during the referendum campaign. I had been fed with so much rubbish over many years that any information showing the EU in a positive light or information showing how leaving would be bad was dismissed by myself out of hand.

A prime example of this is when the government leaflet came through my door. I didn't bother to read it as it was "project fear" anyway, I remember laughing and throwing it in the bin. "We don't need the EU to trade, we can do deals with the rest of the world instead, also two weeks to get a doctors appointment! Less immigrants would make that faster that's for sure!" I thought.

The limited info I did bother to take in proves I was engaging in confirmation bias because I vividly remember sitting and watching videos by Daniel Hannan and Nigel Farage (yuck) and not from any remain campaigner. And those two both convinced me we could have benefits like Norway for example, which has a higher standard of living than us I might add so it seemed plausible to keep economic stability whilst losing the political side.

So I went into the voting booth that day and put my X in the leave box. For some reason, I had this odd feeling of did I do the right thing? I also remember thinking: "Leave won't win anyway, but it should give David Cameron and the EU a shock". Why did I even think that? I'm still not sure but I think it was because I was using the EU as a scapegoat for the issues in my own life.

51

Since the vote, I have been watching it all unfold and the sheer amount of information that has come out since is staggering. How was I or the average person supposed to know about EURATOM, European medicines agency, the inner workings of the EU, our role in it, ERASMUS, Galileo, WTO, schedules, tariffs, origin of manufacturing and on and on. So many things I honestly didn't know about and how could the average person even begin to.

My view on both the EU and immigration has taken a turn since the referendum. Slowly over the years since my biases have been chipped away at by my conscience and the realisation we have all been led up the garden path by people who care not for the wellbeing of us mere peasants but only themselves and their narrow ideology. I can now see that it is not the fault of immigrants that there is a housing shortage or long NHS wait times. I can now see that it is our own government that is to blame, over many years, that the NHS is in the state it is and places like Sunderland and all the other old industrial towns have been left to rot. Nothing to do with the EU at all! And trade, well, I can now see it will be almost suicidal if we become a third country overnight by crashing out. I still have deep reservations about many aspects of the EU as I have learned more about it but the EU has never willingly threatened food and medical shortages, unlike the British government.

In these next few paragraphs, would like to talk about the shame I feel about my vote to leave. I consider myself as British as a bulldog I was born here and my mother is English, but my father and extended family are Italian. I am a complete hypocrite because half of my family are immigrants yet I complained about immigration and voted leave partly due to that viewpoint. My only excuse I can point to is the fact that it was my mothers side of the family that used the immigration slurs growing up and my mum and dad split up when I was a child and didn't see my dad and Italian family for seven years. I lost that connection to my heritage but it doesn't excuse my selfishness.

Also in 2015 my wife was diagnosed with pre-eclampsia whilst pregnant and was admitted to hospital for two weeks. My daughter was born two months early weighing 2.4 pounds and spent two months in the Special Care Baby Unit. She was kept alive by not only British doctors and nurses but EU ones too. I remember one, Andrea, he was a male nurse and he worked 13 hours overnight, went home for a short rest then did a day shift. He helped keep my baby alive with his dedication and compassion and I will always be grateful to him and all the other staff. They are under serious stress doing a job where the wrong choice could mean death.

A demonstration of my selfishness is the fact that I didn't think of those nurses or even my own family who are now subject to registering just to request they can stay here when I voted to leave. And everyday I feel shame.

I'm desperate to change my vote now and my eyes have been opened to the hate peddled by the media and some politicians. I never voted for no deal, I never voted for my family to be treated like outsiders and I never voted for the complete meltdown and neglect of this country.

It's just a shame my eyes have been opened too late.

### Andrew - Acton, West London

I voted to leave because I thought that the UK, not being a member of the Euro, might benefit from a slightly looser relationship with the EU than full membership.

Immigration played no part in my vote to Leave. I was worried about the rise of nationalism, especially after the death of Jo Cox MP, which did make me question whether a vote to leave might fuel xenophobia. But I reflected on this and discussed it with other friends. Eventually I decided that leaving the EU might be a safety valve which by affirming our political independence might reduce nationalistic tensions, which were rising across Europe at that time fuelled by the refugee crisis.

I did not contemplate leaving with No Deal or a deal which damages us. I believed what the Vote Leave campaign and Michael Gove said: it would be easy to get a deal which preserved the economic benefits of the single market and customs union but also enabled us to do our own trade deals around the world.

That was what the government set out as its target – and that matched what Mr Gove had promised. Let's call it "the sunlit uplands vision" or as Mr Gove put it "a happy journey to a better place".

I don't remember ever thinking about or hearing anyone talking about the Irish border. And I was reassured Immediately after the vote, when Boris Johnson said on 26 June 2016, "the UK would still have access to the Single Market" despite Brexit.

I first started to worry in August 2016. I got back to London after a summer holiday and saw hostile behaviour to Europeans; of a kind I had never seen before. "We voted for Brexit – you lot are going home". That sort of thing. And European friends said they had started to feel less welcome here.

Then, watching the Conservative Party Conference in October 2016 I heard, with dismay, Mrs May's nasty rhetoric in her "citizens of nowhere" speech and the proposals announced by Amber Rudd to keep a "register of foreign workers". I found that chilling.

In January 2017, in Theresa May's Lancaster House speech she unveiled her infamous *"red lines"*. This included leaving the single market and ending free movement. This was seriously troubling. She claimed these were what the referendum result *'meant'* but this was just her interpretation: and they were in sharp conflict with my intentions and expectations when voting to leave.

But despite this, a week later on 24 January 2017 David Davies, Brexit Secretary, in a speech in the House of Commons, downplayed the significance of leaving the single market and said he was intending to reach a comprehensive free trade agreement and comprehensive customs agreement that would deliver the *"the exact same benefits as we have but also enable [us] to go and form trade deals with the rest of the world, which is the real upside of leaving the EU"*. That matched what Michael Gove had said. Now of course we can see it is fantasy.

In March 2019, Mrs May triggered Article 50. We now know she had no agreed, credible, or achievable plan.
For some time, I believed, and vociferously argued, that the solution to the Brexit issue was for us to join or re-join the EEA and participate in the Single Market that way; essentially the Norway deal. And I gave vocal support to people like Stephen Kinnock, who advocated that solution.

But as the chaos continued during 2017, I came to see that that that solution did not satisfy either Remainers or harder Brexiteers and that it did not really address my original core concern, because it left us subject to EU regulations but with no voice, no vote and no veto in the formation of regulations or direction of EU travel.

By the end of 2017 it seemed clear to me that the vision promoted by Vote Leave and later David Davies of a deal giving us the "exact same benefits" as we had as members of the EU, but free to do our own trade deals was impossible to achieve.

So eventually, on 22 December 2017 to be precise, I *"came out"* as a RemainerNow.

I was soon contacted by @RemainerNow. I met a group of MPs at the House of Commons, including Anna Soubry and Sam Gyiimah. went on the second Peoples Vote March in 2018 and spoke at the Peoples Vote rally in Westminster. I have made calls to LBC, putting the case for another referendum, and arguing against that it is anti-democratic to deny the electorate the chance to speak again. As Rachel Sylvester said in The Times on 15 October 2019

*"The Brexiteers argue that it would be an affront to democracy to have a second referendum, but the 'will of the people' would not be overturned; rather, the voters would be asked to give their informed consent to a change that was never on the ballot paper in 2016."*

I was a Conservative party member for many years but in 2018 I resigned in protest over its handling of Brexit and immigration. Soon after that I joined the Liberal Democrats. I spoke at a RemainerNow meeting on the fringe of the LibDem party conference in September 2019. I have agreed to attend a RemainerNow meeting with MEPs and Commissioners at the EU Parliament in October 2019.

Since changing my mind, I have thought long and hard about how I made the wrong choice, and why the country is in such a mess. I believe it is the result of a series of deeply flawed decisions by successive governments: Cameron

- In 2013 promising a binary referendum ("a simple in out choice") ignoring the multi-layered complexity of this issue.
- In 2015, setting up that binary referendum but rejecting calls for a super majority on the grounds that the referendum was to be advisory only.
- Promising that the government would implement what "the people" decide, so in effect converting an advisory referendum into a binding referendum.
- Putting a hopelessly general option on the ballot paper. It should have been Remain against a clearly defined Leave alternative, so there would not have been all these argument about what Brexit means.
- Hijacking the undefined Leave vote by interpreting it to mean Hard Brexit.
- Laying down red lines in negotiations which made any sensible deal impossible to achieve.
- Triggering Article 50 without any agreed, workable plan as to what form of relationship with the EU should be achieved.

Looking back, I find it almost incredible that I could, so blithely, have voted to leave the EU, in disregard of all these considerations and persuaded others to do so too. I feel great regret about this but hindsight is a wonderful thing. I believe we have all learnt a great deal since June 2016, and we should all have another chance, but this time much better informed, to express our opinion on this vital issue for our country.

But I was not alone in failing to understand the issues involved: in fact, almost nobody, however well educated, however elite, on either side of the argument understood these issues. No-one knows this better than Dominic Cummings who said in January 2017:

> *"I am not aware of a single MP or political journalist who understands the Single Market – its history, its nature, its dynamics, its legal system, the complex interactions between law, economics, business, history and so on."*

This is a breath-taking indictment of those charged with governing the country at this crucial time. Lessons must be learned from all this: but first, Brexit must be defeated.

**Samual - Dorchester, Dorset**

Confessions of a leave voter

I remember walking to the polling booth on the evening of June 23rd 2016 as if it was yesterday. It was a pleasant evening but my mind was to-ing and fro-ing between leave and remain. I believed at the time that it wouldn't make much difference if we left or remained, that life would go on and the country would continue to be a happy family.

At the time I knew the EU wasn't perfect (I still believe this now), I thought some concessions would benefit us and possibly the EU. I remember David Cameron approaching Brussels with a list of concessions and failing mostly. This nicely leads to my main reasons for voting, I felt like a close vote in remains favour would fire a warning shot to the EU and perhaps in the future, concessions would be delivered.

I also considered ticking the leave box as a protest vote against the establishment. I felt disillusioned with politics and the government, I never felt like my voice was heard or I was represented. I was tired of the same type of "suit" becoming Prime Minister and claiming to represent us when seemingly all they did for young people was increase tuitions fee and very little else.

On the morning of the 24th I instantly turned on my TV, I was surprised by the news and surprised by my reaction. I felt like I had just eaten a takeaway which was enjoyable at the time but instantly regrettable. Whilst I was sad and regretted the whole situation, I wasn't yet cursing myself. I still felt that it wouldn't make much difference.

For a couple years it did not seem real, it felt like we would never leave then unfortunately I found myself in intensive care fighting for my life. I realised that the tax I had paid over numerous years had not been wasted but mostly with my new found boredom (I was off work for months), I had to find a new source of entertainment. I stumbled across a radio station with a brilliant host who continually called out the lies of leave, you can probably guess who. My understanding of Brexit increased and simultaneously my passion and respect for remain and the EU did too. Through the research I was conducting daily alongside listening to the radio, I was no longer to-ing and fro-ing, I knew Brexit was damaging and I knew I was ardently against it. I began campaigning for a second referendum, supporting remain parties and I had hope that this country would see through the lies. I had finally learned why I had "takeaway regret" on the morning of the 24th.

Fast forward to today and the regret, sadness and frustration has continued to develop daily, I hope it has peaked because I do not want to feel any worse about the decision than I do today writing this. To me it has become clear that we were lied to and that Brexit is an awful idea. The signs were there in 2016, I just failed to see them. My only hope from this episode in British history is that we never allow ourselves to be fooled again although I suspect we haven't learned our lesson.

I reflect on myself as a person in 2016, my vote and general understanding and I am extremely proud of how far I have come as a person. None of what I said at the beginning really made sense to me then, it certainly does not now. I read recently that a key concept to understanding life is to objectively realise that we see life subjectively and not subjectively objectively. When one removes the tinted glasses, we can finally realise that immigration has not been bad for this country, that through the single market we have access to the largest trading block in the world, a ban on bendy bananas, free ports etc and many other reasons are just nonsense. I still to this day await a tangible benefit and I have asked 100s of leave voters.

For now I will continue to hold this government to account but I look forward to the re-join campaign, whenever that is.

# PART THREE
## RemainerNow Articles from 'Politics Means Politics' website
Visit them on their website: pmp-magazine.com


## Hugh

This piece was written by Hugh, from the South West of England, who in-spired #RemainerNow to start their campaign to share stories of Leave voters who have now reconsidered Brexit.

*First published in July 2018.*


I voted Leave in the 2016 referendum and have since changed my mind. Here I set out why I voted leave in the first place and why, knowing so much more than I did in 2016, I'm a Remainer now and wish to remain a full member of the EU.

I do this in the knowledge that there are many in a similar position and with the objective to encourage them to speak up and to add their voice for a People's Vote on the final Brexit deal, with the option to remain as full members of the EU.

Before the Referendum
Prior to 2016 I had never really thought much about the EU. Indeed, the only time I was vaguely aware of it was when, on the rare occasion it did make the news, it was generally in either a negative ('red tape central bur-eaucracy holding back business') or comical ('bendy bananas') context – 1 or 2 rare minutes of a news bulletin was about the maximum coverage it received.

Never prior to 2016 (that I am aware of) did the British public have any objective and informed insight into what the EU is, how it came to be, what is represents, how it works, how we play our part in it and what benefits membership brings to our daily lives and that of business. In the months leading up to the referendum I therefore sought to better understand the EU as best I could.

A decision on whether to remain or leave the EU was not something I had ever considered, requested, wanted or needed. I also didn't appreciate being asked to answer such an important question for which I was not qualified or had the tools/information to answer, but it was something I took seriously.

## The Role of the Media

Many who voted to leave are accused of not doing their homework, but I know this is not the case. There were of course good journalists and journalism out there during this period, but in general the mainstream media's coverage of the Referendum debate was often reduced to 'infotainment' rather than insightful and informed factual analysis.

I was not a Twitter user at that time, so the BBC was my main source of information. It pains me to say that I feel it let the public down significantly in their coverage; something Nick Cohen encapsulated so well in his excellent article.

I listened intently to both campaigns, followed the debates, documentaries and commentaries, but the media's constant emphasis on balance between claim and counter-claim, regardless of the facts or how one claim/fact had more impact than another, led me to believe there really was nothing between the campaigns and by the end of the campaigning I was unsure who or what to believe.

## Quality of the Campaigns

After the debates were over I was faced with making my decision. I felt the Remain campaign did nothing to sell any positive representation of the EU and benefits of membership. It was a very negative campaign, only emphasising the down-sides of leaving (dismissed by the Leave campaign as 'Project Fear'), but none of the benefits of staying.

The Leave campaign on the other hand were selling a positive message of 'no down-sides, only up-sides', the 'exact same benefits' as now, additional global trade (which we were told was not possible as EU members), more money for our public services (the NHS in particular) and the fact that this would be a quick and easy deal in both the UK's and EU's interests.
Just as importantly there was no talk of using people as bargaining chips or reducing people's rights, which I would never have thought possible for consideration of any UK Government.

I also believe that the fact we were told by the Chancellor at the time that there would be an 'emergency budget' the day after the referendum if Leave won, lost the Remain campaign credibility and added to the negative perception of it.

As Femi Oluwole (Our Future Our Choice) put it so well, the general emphasis of the Remain campaign was 'vote for us or the zombies will come out'. Hardly an inspiring vision to be asked to rally behind.

Decision Time
On the morning of the vote I was faced between a decision of 'better the devil you know' from the Remain campaign or giving the Leave campaign a chance to deliver what they were claiming.

It was a very difficult decision, but I eventually opted for Leave to see if they could realise their claims. Given the fact that we were presented with a binary decision, this was the only way of finding out if their vision was possible. Naïve this may have been, but I made the decision based on the information in front of me at the time.

Of course, in hindsight I realise what a mistake this was. It is now clear the Leave claims were based on lies and misinformation which are undeliverable and have crumbled in the face of reality.

I, like many regretful Leave voters, feel misled, misinformed and 'played' by the Leave campaign in order to obtain our vote.

Interpretation of Vote
As I saw the interpretation of the Leave win morph into one which stated the people had voted to leave the single market and customs union, the 'back-pedalling' over the promises of more money for our public services, using people as bargaining chips and reducing their rights and the fuelling of xenophobic behaviour, I was horrified.

I would never have believed any UK Government would interpret the vote in this way when it would so obviously damage the country, polarise public opinion, put people's lives and jobs at risk and make so many feel unwelcome in a country that has thrived from their contributions.

While for some immigration was a factor in their decision, this was not the case for me or many other leave voters, who have always seen immigration as a positive for the country, and which makes it the best it can be. I still believe the vast majority of the UK public are open and welcoming.

Our media's narrative and that of many politicians of 'Freedom of Movement' still seems focused only on workers entering the UK and not the many UK workers in mainland Europe. They seem intent on portraying migration in a negative light rather than highlighting the necessity of it and the benefits it brings to any country.

After the vote I saw David Cameron resign, most of the Leave campaigners too and then a leadership contest which led to an interpretation of the vote into something I would never have voted for. It was at this point I realised I needed to speak up and that I could not be alone in my resistance to how my vote was being interpreted.

Now Better Informed
Since reducing my reliance on mainstream media news and making connections with knowledgeable sources and institutions through social media, I have since learned so much more about the EU with information I did not have available to me at the time of the Referendum.

I used to think the Referendum decision was simply about economics and believed that economics always finds a way, as this was generally the thread of most debates.

However, I've since learned how the EU came to be and its many benefits, from helping to sustain peace in Europe, protecting the environment, offering the freedom to travel, work and live in 27 other countries.

Regarding immigration, I learnt how the UK always had full control of its borders and how other EU countries implement border policies which are available to us, despite the myth perpetuated during the referendum.

Other benefits too such as no mobile roaming fees, protection of worker's rights, membership of Euratom, Space and Satellite programmes, the European Medicines Agency which helps research into new drugs and Open Skies which has led to cheaper air fares; to name but a few.

Indeed, the more I learned about the EU, its benefits, our contribution to its policies and our freedoms within it, the more I realise that, despite the fact it is not perfect and constantly needs reform (like any organisation), the phrase 'Take Back Control' was no more than an effective marketing slogan.

As full EU members, it's us working with our European partners who are setting the rulebook and it's clearer than ever that we never lost control, so there was never anything to take back.

The benefits of our EU membership, which the UK contributed so much to shaping, are so numerous, I fail to understand now how any Government could have felt a referendum on it was ever needed and I truly believe that this was an internal debate within the Conservative party which spiralled out of control.

In addition, how it could have been reduced to a binary question outsourced to the unqualified public is, in beyond comprehension.

If only we had all the correct information in 2016, if we understood the benefits, if the Remain campaign was more positive, if the media fully informed the public and exposed misinformation about the EU during the referendum. But alas, we are where we are.

The Will of the People?
The general interpretation in Westminster and among many political journalists is "The People Have Voted", it is the "Will of the People" and democracy demands that we must implement it, regardless of the damage it will do (and has already done even though we have not left yet) to the country and to UK/EU citizens.

As someone who voted Leave I say this is not the case.

This Government has debated for 2 years about what Brexit is, means and looks like and they still cannot agree between themselves. It is therefore not feasible for any Government to claim they know what people voted for in 2016. I know that their interpretation of my vote is incorrect, as we were sold nothing but upsides, not the shambles we are currently faced with. We voted on a false prospectus which cannot be delivered and cannot be sustained. Added to this, we were told this referendum was advisory and how many people therefore took the opportunity to send a message of defiance to the sitting Government; a message to tell them they feel forgotten, regardless of the question in front of them?

With the information we had available at the time, it is simply not accurate or feasible to say the public made an informed decision based on the facts. As has been said; it was a binary vote on a rainbow of issues.

In addition, every piece of Government analysis since the vote has shown that there are only 'least worst' options, rather than the positive vision we were sold in 2016. The electoral commission has since confirmed that Vote Leave did indeed break electoral law and business is increasingly speaking up about the impending damage that Brexit will cause. Far from achieving 'Global Britain' (as if we were not global already), our standing in the world is diminishing.

This can no longer be dismissed as 'Project Fear', but is now 'Project Fact'. How can any sitting Government actively pursue a policy which, despite what we were told in 2016, has been proven to damage the country?

So What Now?
So where do we go from here? My personal preference is for Westminster to show leadership and put the country's interest first. To explain to the public that they have tried to come up with a good deal but that, based on the evidence now available, it is not possible without causing significant damage to the country and to people's lives. To therefore to stop Brexit and remain and reform within the EU.

However, I appreciate this would cause much upset to those who still want to leave the EU regardless of its ramifications. Similarly, a 'Norway' style deal or full 'Hard Brexit' WTO/No Deal would cause similar upset to those with opposing views.

It's over 2 years since the referendum and the debates, arguments and interpretations of what the vote meant still go on. In the meantime, Brexit continues to absorb the Government's focus, preventing progress on many of the issues which contributed to the Leave vote in the first place.

An Informed Choice with a Clear Mandate
At the heart of democracy is trust in those who Govern, but trust must be earned. I and many others trusted those politicians who claimed leaving the EU would be beneficial to the country without any negative impact to either its UK or EU citizens. The evidence now available, including from the Government itself, proves that this trust has been breached.

All of the above leads me to believe the only way to resolve this situation is for the Government to conclude its negotiations and then offer a choice back to the people between the deal it strikes and remaining as full EU members.

This would once and for all put the facts in front of the people – an informed decision giving an informed mandate, whatever the result. No more 'claim and counter claim' or reliance on interpretations and no more arguments about it being "the best of 3" if the result is different – just the real facts allowing for a fully informed decision and mandate.

This is the only way, in my view, to truly know what the will of the people is and why I and so many others who voted Leave in 2016 now support a 'People's Vote' on the final deal, with the option to remain as full EU members.

After all, what could be more democratic than offering the people a vote on the facts, on the truth? The future of the country and its future generations is at stake. It's time to end the divisions once and for all and restore trust in our democratic system with a People's Vote.

# Simranjeet

Simranjeet, an equity research analyst who is also working on groundbreaking tech to treat dementia and anxiety, explains his current views of his Leave vote two years on.

Just over two years ago, I reluctantly made the decision to vote for Britain to leave the European Union. I have regretted that decision severely. I'm a 22-year-old adult, I need to take responsibility for my actions and admit I was wrong. Hopefully, inside this article, you'll have a full accounting of my thought process during the referendum, why I changed my mind and what I believe Britain and the European Union must do, moving forward, to heal the divisions caused by the process.

Before I expand any further, I want to emphasise a crucial point. I am not a xenophobe, nor am I someone who subscribes to the nauseating phenomenon of nascent populism that has emerged globally within the last 4 years. I am a First generation immigrant, born in East London to parents who migrated from India in the early 1990s. I grew up with many friends of different backgrounds. I take pride in a diverse Britain. I am emphasising this because I will commonly be referring to the principle of 'possibility' in regards to Brexit. I have talked to people who are xenophobic and/or populists. This crucial sentiment of 'possibility' is important to understand how disparate the Brexit supporting coalition at the time was.

When the referendum campaign began, I started off as a reluctant Remain supporter. I was reasonably satisfied with the renegotiations that the Cameron ministry had secured with the European Union, however, I had no affection for the bureaucracy that ran the commission. Like most people in the U.K., we were constantly being told about the inefficiencies within Brussels and the occasional ECJ ruling that may be antithetical towards British interests. The commission was never our friend, rather a group of technocrats (or Eurocrats as was a common saying) that seemed determined at all opportunities to hinder innovation.

At the approximate time of the referendum, the EU was not doing well. It was plagued by lethargic economic growth and seemed to hobble from one political and economic crisis to the next. The EU-Canadian free trade deal seemed to take an excruciatingly long time to conclude due to some holdovers within smaller countries. However, I knew that staying within the economic block, of which we had been a part of for 41 years, seemed like the sensible thing to do.

Now, before I get onto what was the main catalyst for me changing my vote I think I should at least provide an additional bit of context. I was best friends at the time with an ardent Leave supporter. His main claim to leave was regarding the argument of sovereignty. He specifically said that he didn't care about the economic damage it would cause. We had several long discussions about Brexit and its philosophy. His passionate conviction to leave was much stronger than my tepid desire to remain and I slowly started sympathising to his views. Now, we are no longer on talking terms, let alone friends, having fallen out over something completely unrelated to Brexit.

What ultimately made me change my mind, was a debate held by my university where Anne Milton was hosting, whilst Anna Soubry faced off against Douglas Carswell. Throughout the debate, I was thoroughly unimpressed with Ms. Soubry's arguments to remain. She started off by talking about the Second World War and recycling the most negative talking points from the Remain campaign. Mr. Carswell, however, provided an extremely optimistic picture of Britain post-European Union. He emphasised how we would be able to immediately secure a free trade agreement with the European Union whilst being free to pursue Free Trade Agreements (FTAs) at our own prerogative. Which meant we could enter into an FTA with the United States, ASEAN, potentially enter the TPP. Whilst keeping the existing trade relationship with the EU. We would have immigration from across the world of workers who were diverse but now highly skilled. Essentially it was global Britain.

The idea was incredibly appealing to me at the time. This is now where I hark back to the theme of possibility. For me, Brexit was the opportunity to have more globalism, more free trade, to integrate ourselves further within the global economy. I imagined a Britain with even more immigration from workers in the fields of science, technology, art, finance. With my finance and technology background, I imagined it would be easier to do business with countries across the globe. At the same time, we would remove ourselves from the bureaucracy of the 'unelected cabal' of the European Commission. Europe was a mess, its prospects at the time seemed dim. We were part of a quasi-federation which didn't know whether it wanted to be a Superstate or an economic union.

Mr. Carswell also raised two questions which I erroneously subscribed too:
1. Would you vote to join the European Union today if we weren't part of it, based on how different it has become since 1975?

2. Why does Europe not have its own Silicon Valley?

That debate and those two questions were enough for me to change my mind. So four weeks later, I voted to leave. The polls were deadlocked, so I had no idea what to expect, though I had reasonable hope my side would win. Lo and behold we did.

In the ensuing months, it seemed that I had made the right choice for the most part. The country had a cabinet that seemed to want to deliver a Brexit that was essentially global Britain. The EU-Canada free trade deal teetered on the verge of collapse because the parliament of Wallonia remained intransigent on it. Donald Trump was elected President, he promised that Britain would be "front of the queue" for any FTA.
For the first few months this made Brexit seem like a boon for the country, and then it all changed...

My vision of Brexit clearly was not the vision of Brexit that others shared. Where I wanted free trade, others wanted protectionism. Where I wanted more immigration, others wanted nativism. Where I wanted cooperation with the European Union, others wanted hostility. The rise in racist incidents were extremely troubling, giving light to a more ugly side within our society.

The European Union will naturally need to protect their own interests, to expect them to capitulate towards all of our demands would have been fanciful. Like I mentioned before, immigration was not a concern for me, the volume of data supported claims that EU immigration was beneficial to the country.
It took me until roughly this time last year to realise that what I had voted for was not going to be delivered. I felt I had been lied to. Plain and simple. Or perhaps I hadn't been lied to, rather I had simply voted for something neither I nor anyone truly knew. Once more I talk about the possibility, for me, I saw the opportunity to transform the UK into a further services economy, based on finance, technology, and entertainment. For others, it was a chance to double down on an outdated products market, restore dangerous tariffs and impose a foreboding and xenophobic immigration system. Often the refrain of "Get rid of the foreigners" was said.

I also realised the answer to one of Mr. Carswell's questions: that Europe doesn't have one singular Silicon Valley... it has multiple smaller ones.
As the negotiation process drew on, I did not anticipate the complete incompetence of Her Majesty's Government in negotiating with itself on its

ideal of Brexit and then carrying that over to the European Union. We now stand on the precipice of crashing out of the European Union and reverting back to archaic World Trade Organisation (WTO) rules.

The fact is plain and simple, the reality has changed. Leaving is now the de-facto position of the government. They will have no deal. Leaving without any agreement and the economic impact it would have was never part of the Leave platform. The cabal of hard Brexiteers in parliament, the European Research Group (ERG) and their amendments have essentially made it such that the EU will reject a deal due to the asinine nature of their demands. Even if by happenstance an arrangement could be arranged, it would inevit-ably be tantamount to colonial status giving us one of the worst possible arrangement for Britain's future, save for leaving without any arrangement.

Once again, this was not remotely close to what I voted for. If I had known the outcome we were heading towards, I would have voted emphatically to remain. With my work in finance and technology, with what I want to do. Leaving the United Kingdom to pursue my efforts, would be more prefer-able than living within the confines of an isolated island that inflicted no-deal upon itself by its government.

So, now, I believe that as the terms of our departure from the European Union are becoming clearer it is time for us to have a referendum on the final deal: as a nation do we truly want to leave our political and economic partners for the void of uncertainty?

Earlier, I mentioned one question Mr. Carswell asked, "Would you vote to join the European Union today, based on how different it is when we joined?" That question, I realise now, was irrelevant because joining a polit-ical union is vastly different from staying part of one. So, now, I'd like to ask the question: Would you vote to leave the European Union today based on how different the circumstances are to when you voted to leave in 2016? For me and many others, I suspect that the answer would be NO.

I know that to suggest a referendum will be billed as heresy to the demo-cratic principles we pride ourselves on in the West. However, the notion that the 'will of the people' is immutable as they learn more information is pre-posterous, arrogant and dangerous. Was it a betrayal of the will of the people to hold the 2016 referendum when the people had chosen by an overwhelming margin to remain in 1975? Was it a betrayal of the will of the people to suggest that in the event of a Remain victory, Leave groups would continue campaigning for a withdrawal? Is it a betrayal of the will of the people, now that polls show the people would prefer a referendum, to hold one?

We must resist the overwhelming noise from the likes of Nigel Farage or Jacob Rees-Mogg. Whilst I can admire their conviction in doing what they earnestly believe, they are simply wrong in what a hard Brexit will entail. In truth, their ideal version of Brexit will cause undue harm. When Mr. Rees-Mogg says we may not realise the potential of Brexit for 50 years he says this because he is indifferent to the damage it will cause the public. Mr. Mogg and the likes of the ERG will be fine, we in the public will not.

I would go so far to argue that if they succeed in their efforts, in establishing a hard no deal Brexit. Mr. Farage, Rees-Mogg and the hard Brexiteers will have succeeded in doing what General Bonaparte or Kaiser Wilhelm II or any of Britain's historical enemies had failed to do. They would have sub-jugated Britain and damaged it irreparably.

No one should feel ashamed to change their minds. Most people that voted for Brexit did so because they legitimately felt that they were improving the future of Britain. Instead of animosity, a reasonable dialogue should be made for people such as myself that evolved their position and the millions that are on the fence about it now.

A referendum will most likely be a close affair. I believe that Brexit did have one advantage, it laid bare the soul of this nation and of the European Union. The European Union has echoed repeatedly that we could cancel this entire sordid affair and resume like business as usual. The truth is, in the event of remaining, we won't have fully resolved the longstanding issues that led us to initially leave, neither will it solve the ascendency of populism in European Union's constituent states.
We must do more. We must reform Europe…

In the event of remaining, Britain needs to take a leading role within the European project. No more half in and half out uncertainty. We must fix the problems that we have within Europe, instead of cowering behind exemp-tions we must see further integration as the opportunity to shape the destiny of Europe. In the most recent meeting between European heads of states, Chancellor Merkel praised our contribution, lamenting her regret that we were leaving. Prime Minister Rutte of the Netherlands has expressed a sim-ilar sentiment regarding our departure. We have proven that when we have a vested interest in Europe, when we care about the direction of this Union, we can push in a direction that aligns with our interests and values.

I'd like to state that if there was any political party that most aligned with my views, it would be the Freie Demokratische Partei, or Free Democratic Party (FDP), in Germany. I truly believe that by employing the values of classical liberalism to maximise social and economic liberty, our peoples will be given the opportunity to succeed based upon their merit. This could be a model for a reformed European Union.

The most pressing change we can fix is that of the European Commission, we have within our power to make the President of Europe an elected position. Conceivably, we may one day have a candidate from Île-de-France against a candidate from Bavaria debate in front of a studio audience in Warsaw in English.

To become more efficient and for the European Union to reach the aspirations of its citizens we must seriously consider fully integrating. We cannot allow the European Union to remain this quasi-state. If I was ever privileged enough to talk with President Macron, I'm sure he and the movement he started would be the most receptive to transforming the European Union.

To list every conceivable reform would take too long. So I'll end with this. The European Union has improved the lives of its citizens through being part of it. The aspirations of its people depend on living within a system that can respond to its needs. We must integrate more to thrive, where we can together create a Union that can set an example across Earth to promote our sacred values of liberty and rule of law to provide justice and tranquillity for all.

# Steve

Steve's story is the one of a man from Cornwall who, against all odds, over-came adversity time and time again thanks to the NHS. Steve explains how he feels about the lies that led him to vote Leave two years ago and why he now wants a People's Vote.

I was born in 1961. I was a breech birth, my poor old mother was 48 hours in labour with me, and she had a hard time of it. I was a difficult birth. Eventually, I was delivered by forceps. I was not expected to survive, but emergency transfusions and the hard work of the NHS saved my life. I was three days old before my mother saw me for the first time.

On 19 January 1981, I had a serious motorcycle accident, spent some time in hospital and couldn't see properly from my right eye for about six weeks. Yet again, the NHS saved my life.

19 years ago, I was diagnosed with diabetes. Yep, you guessed it: the NHS keeps me alive today. So, when the Leave campaign sold its lie of £350 million boost for the NHS, who wouldn't have voted for it?

The thing is 'that' NHS lie was a calculated lie. They knew it was never going to happen; they looked for something; they knew it would gain votes. It was something they knew people like me who love our NHS would not resist; they never intended to carry it through. It was nothing but a cynical scam.

Brexit was to be easy and great for the country. We were all to be better off, the NHS was going to boom, there was going to be no downside.
Again, this was nothing but a cynical lie.

The truth is that the Leave campaign STOLE my vote, they scammed me and many others out of something precious, something people died to gain the right to.
They stole our votes.

If Boris Johnson had called people up and scammed them out of their bank details, he would now be locked up. He scammed us out of our votes, and what happened to him? They made him Foreign Secretary. Then, he gets a high-paid job writing for a so-called "newspaper." (Editor's note: The Tele-graph)

Now, here we are in 2018. The reality of Brexit is clear: we are all going to be worse off. We have a "food supply minister", Michael Gove wants to open-up dumps so people can scavenge. Workers rights are for the chop, and food standards have to go to get food from the United States. It's a step backwards 50 years.

That's not what we were sold. It's not what we voted for. The truth is that their "fantasy" Brexit was never achievable.

I say give us EVERYTHING you promised, or give us the chance to change our minds.
No one can know the "Will of the People" today in 2018, unless the people are asked again.
Democracy did not end in 2016. Or did it?

# Josh

Josh voted Leave two years ago. He had time to think again and has now changed his mind. No doubt in his mind: he wants a People's Vote.

Imagine voting in a general election. You go into the ballot box, but this time there are only two options. The question reads "Do you want to change the governing party?"
Yes.
No.
You make your mark next to 'Yes' and stroll out of the ballot box happy with your decision.

At no point were you asked which party you would like to be in power. No one was. There are parties A, B, C, D and E to pick from and the current government hasn't got a clue what people voted for, so they guess.

A general election would never be run this way, so why is it that the Brexit referendum was? No one was asked how they wanted to leave. Or at what cost. The government, at best, are guessing.

It explains why the Tories can't agree with themselves, everyone's guess is different, and why there are so many versions of Brexit, with the supporters of each claiming they represent 'the will of the people'. Options include chequers, no deal, Canada+++, Norway style and full unicornist.

Whereas there's only one version of Remain. Categorically and unequivocally, the support for Remain is far greater than the support for any individual version of Brexit.

Will of the people.
Speaking of the will of the people... It's not, is it?
For a referendum to be binding, a majority for change needs to be well in excess of 52%. So, either it is binding, in which case the result wasn't high enough for Leave to enact the change, or it is advisory.

Furthermore, citizens from a number of EU countries that may have lived here for decades leading up to the vote, but didn't seek British citizenship as they had EU citizenship (ergo saw no need for it, until now) were denied a vote. These are the people, our neighbours, our friends, who will likely be the most affected. Yet, they had no voice...

How about the thousands of British citizens living abroad who were also denied a vote? Or the 16 and 17-year olds (who are ironically now old enough to vote) who will be living with the fallout from a decision made by their parents and grandparents?

The will of the people is actually the will of 37% of the people in June 2016.

And it's been hijacked.2017 General election result.
Let's address this myth too. The general election result in 2017 does not represent a mandate for Brexit in any way.

Both main parties stood on a promise to enact Brexit. It's the largest single issue in politics, yes, but IT IS STILL A SINGLE ISSUE.

It wasn't a re-run of the Brexit referendum; it was to decide who runs the country. Any party standing on a manifesto promising to stop Brexit is not going to win everyone's vote if the rest of the manifesto is terrible.

There's much more to play for in a general election. Otherwise, the current government should assume nothing else from their manifesto is important or has any support from the public.
They can't have it both ways.

Lies.
Vote Leave broke the electoral law, according to the Electoral Commission. You were lied to; we were all lied to. We were victims. But normally, if you are lied to, you have the right to change your mind.

If you buy something, but later find out it's not what's advertised on the box, you can take it back.

"But the Remain campaign lied too…" Two wrongs don't make a right. In fact, it's even more justification that the campaign was illegitimate!

Shift in opinions.
Polls are consistently saying the UK is #RemainerNow. The lead that Remain has over Leave has been put as high as 1.9 million very recently, higher than the 1.3 million lead the Leave vote achieved in 2016.

This is fuelled by many more voters switching from Leave to Remain than vice versa. The traffic is almost entirely one way (with the exception of Tory party faithful falling in with the party line).

What next?
Simple. A People's Vote. Do we want whatever the government has agreed, no deal or to Remain? Those are the three options on the table.
Don't let anyone tell you we can't undo this mess. Article 50 can be cancelled, as said by the author of Article 50 himself.
The EU won't stop us cancelling the whole thing. They've said it on many occasions: Brexit is regrettable and the door is still wide open.

Despite the Brexiteers' propaganda, the EU is not some horrible dictatorship with a grudge against Britain.
It's time we look again at this madness and decide whether it's what we really want.
After voting Leave in 2016, I am now a committed #RemainerNow pushing for a People's Vote on the final deal for Brexit. Join me!

# Chris

This is an Open Letter written by Chris, from Essex. Chris voted Leave in 2016. He has since changed his mind and wants a People's Vote so that he can now vote for Britain to Remain in the European Union.

Dear Members of Parliament,

As the momentum behind a final say on whatever deal the Prime Minister brings back gathers pace, some still talk of the electorate as though it was frozen in time on 23rd June 2016, that no one has changed their minds since.

I'm one such voter who has changed his mind, and from personal experience, and the efforts of groups like RemainerNow on social media, I can confidently say I am not alone.

I recently had the opportunity to sit in a committee room in Parliament in front of MPs from both sides of the House, with a diverse cross section of other people who voted to leave the EU, and have now, on reflection, changed their minds.

From NHS workers, to the self-employed, to signallers working on our rail network and to a former volunteer at Vote Leave, we come from all walks of life, and from across the political spectrum. We all voted for what at the time, we thought was for the good of the country.

Over two years on from that vote, we have seen a government fail to address any of the drivers behind the decision to leave, and we have seen them, and on many occasions the Opposition treat them like one group, with one goal and with one vision for the UK.

We've seen promises made during the referendum broken without shame, and we've seen to our horror, a country and its politics lurch worryingly to the far-right. We've seen our international reputation damaged, and we've seen that the notion of trading with the rest of the world on favourable terms to be a fallacy.

While there are many who celebrate the above course of events, there are many who don't, and now reject the idea of leaving the EU as a result. However, this isn't about Remain versus Leave, or which side would win in a vote on the final deal. At its heart it's about democracy and informed consent.

Just over two years ago 52% of the electorate asked the government to find us a new home, and we all deserve to see what they come back with before we sign any contract. With such a diverse electorate from across the political spectrum, there can be no Brexit deal that satisfies the wishes of everyone who voted for it, and for every vote to leave the EU, there was a different version of what that should look like.

We understand that at every election political parties make promises that for whatever reason, sometimes can't be kept. The referendum, however, was built on promises that were meant to be broken, and that stains our democracy. Let's not forget; there wouldn't even be a campaign for a People's Vote if the promises made during the referendum were being kept.

Give the nation the opportunity to look at the final deal, and judge for itself whether or not it meets the expectations of 2016. If the majority looks at the deal on offer, and compares it to what was promised and decides that it matches up and is the best route for jobs, workers' rights, the NHS, the environment and more, then we will still leave anyway, but we will be able to confidently say that the electorate knew what they were going to get.

Perhaps then we can begin the process of healing a divided country. If however, the majority look at the deal and reject it in favour of staying in the EU, then we should all sigh with relief that we checked before jumping.

Finally, I would implore all of you to ask yourselves these two questions when making your decision when the deal comes back to Parliament and the prospect of a People's Vote is raised:
• "Will leaving on these terms genuinely improve the lives of my constituents and fix the problems with the country?"
• "Am I 100% sure this is still supported by a majority of the electorate?"
If there is any doubt in the answer to either of these questions, give it back to the people and allow us all to make the final decision ourselves.

Yours sincerely,
Chris,
A voter who has changed his mind.

# David

David, a 56-year-old former NHS consultant from North East Somerset, voted Leave in 2016. He has now changed his mind and wants another referendum to vote Remain.

Before being an NHS Consultant working in a major centre specialising in new-born intensive care, I was a university lecturer and research scientist. In my work I had the privilege of looking after sick and dying babies and their families from all over Britain, Europe, and many other parts of the world.

I have worked with some amazing colleagues from many, many countries. I also helped set up a small charity to support health and education in a village in a Muslim country in sub-Saharan Africa.

My grandparents and great uncles all fought in the last two world wars, and freedom and democracy are hugely important to me.

For me, the EU is undemocratic because I can't vote for a member of the European parliament personally. This is because in EU elections you vote for a person under a regional party list system. Also because the EU ignores referendums results and asks people to vote again (until they come up with the right answer) or the EU just carries on anyway. That's why I voted leave in 2016.

But when voting in a democracy, we should be given the facts and the truths to make an informed decision that chimes with our thoughts and values. This did not happen in the EU Referendum of 2016. Instead we were fed lies, half-truths, and promises that could never be delivered.

I was also naïve: I believed that politicians would look after the rights of us ordinary people and not use people as bargaining chips or currency. Instead, many of our friends, colleagues, partners and their families' lives are in limbo: not knowing what is going to happen to them in the future.

For example, I recently heard a German lady speak about this. She had never stood up in public before and expressed how painful this was for her and her family. She has been married to an Englishman for 25 years. He served in the British army, including three campaigns, and was posted all over Europe.

Being a military-wife, she endured poor accommodation, not knowing when or if her husband would be coming home and supported her family. In her way doing her bit for Queen and Country. But because she has lived out of the UK for much of her married life and does not have an income she does still not know if she will be able to live in the UK after Brexit with her family.

Also, I did not know that some British citizens living in the EU were denied the right to vote in the Referendum.

And why were people who came in good faith from Europe denied a vote in the Referendum? They came to work in the UK and set up good lives, businesses, contribute to society and pay their taxes. What is fair about taxation without representation?

Instead, peoples' lives are being torn apart: many who didn't even have a say, and we have a Brexit "deal" that almost no-one would have voted for in the Referendum.

## Oliver

Oliver, an A-Level student, writer and campaigner, Editor at The People's News, voted Leave in 2016. But after thinking carefully about the ramifications of Brexit, he has changed his mind and is now a committed Remainer. He explains why.

My transition from foolishly supporting Brexit to realising that our future depends entirely on the European Union...

When we discovered that the UK had decided to leave, I thought, "Wow, the people have invoked change; asserted their superiority over governance and given the establishment something to sweat over."

What a fool I was. And as time passed and I realised the political and economic ramifications of such a crucial vote, I experienced the first ever symptom of political nausea. Soon, I became fed up with the 'will of the people' mantra.

For me, I realised: What an absurd and regressive decision to hold a referendum on such an issue. Referendums are proven to never solve an issue, but merely exacerbate tension and conflict.

It became clear that, rather than taking control of our future, we had committed an act of political suicide; rejecting cultural pluralism, cooperation and trade in pursuit of some lofty superpower nostalgia and toxic provincialism.

Indeed, rather than try to reform the European Union's manifold shortcomings in a bi-lateral manner, we simply decided to cede and retreat into isolationism with delusions of national autonomy in a globalised world.

What people need to realise is that we need the European Union as much as it requires us. We must retain our ability to shape international policy directives, our ability to share information, resources, talent, education. Whatever its flaws, we can work together to reform the EU.

# Gary

A student at the University of Essex and a Green Party member, Gary from Norwich voted Leave in 2016. Considering now that he didn't know enough to vote one way or the other, he has changed his mind. A Remainer now, he wants a People's Vote.

Initially, my vote for Britain to leave the EU was simply a reaction to how poorly the government was conducting the negotiations. However, having considered the issue, I have come to appreciate the many and varied ways the UK is enhanced by EU membership.

My decision to vote leave wasn't particularly influenced by the referendum campaign. I had become so disillusioned by the quality of debate that much of it passed me by. My decision to support Leave was a result of deep-seated ideological influence constructed over many years.

Why did I fall for the narrative spun by eurosceptic politicians and a complicit media — a narrative of a once proud nation, held back by the EU, having ceded its sovereignty? I can't for the life of me see the appeal of leaving now. I never hated the EU. I felt European.

I was always comfortable describing myself as English, British and European. I certainly never felt superior. Maybe I have put critical distance between myself and the invidious lies about the European Union that fuel euroscepticism and dislike of the EU.

Was it a sense of nostalgia for a time that once existed, but no longer does? I honestly don't know now. It is possible that I never fully believed in it and only now do I feel able to articulate my actual views. Whatever it is, I didn't know enough to vote one way or the other.

The information was out there. I could have listened to Ken Clarke instead of Daniel Hannan. I could have read more widely... no, I should have! But that is all in the past now. I try to understand why people still advocate for Brexit, despite the knowledge of what it means. I thought Remainers needed to show compassion and understanding, that eventually the majority of people would come to their senses when it became clear that Brexit carried significant costs. A smaller economy. Food and medicine shortages. A diminished role in the world.

I thought cold hard evidence would win out and the Leave argument would collapse under the weight of its own incongruity. I now realise that this was misguided. For many the Brexit narrative is so engrained that nothing will budge it. This is the challenge.

To people who might say: 'Sorry Gary, but I get quite angry at people like you. You should have known better. Your careless vote has put us where we are now,' I say: that is fine. You are entitled to your opinion and, by God, I have been pretty pissed at myself for quite a while now. However, you should try to understand how an anti-EU narrative that has persisted in Britain over the duration of our membership of the European Union has influenced the way millions voted.

Implying a lack of intelligence or foresight rather underplays the way ideology works is wrong. I still believe there were good faith reasons to vote to Leave, but have come to accept that they were all based on faulty logic. The UK is poorer because of Brexit. Our political system is broken and our politicians, largely incompetent. Yes, we still have borders, and our attitude towards those outside them is an embarrassment to us. My vote to leave was a mistake.

I am not seeking sympathy; just the opportunity to amend my 2016 vote. The way EU nationals have been treated was not inevitable and was/is completely unnecessary. The young have so much to lose from leaving the EU. They will be a major influence on the outcome of a future vote.
I have significantly revised my political views in the last 2.5 years and one major aspect has been a greater focus on environmental issues. I now appreciate that we are much better placed to tackle these issues in a unified response than individually.

I think we now need to make a positive case for Remain, rather than just arguing about the negative consequences of leaving the EU. It is important that we start to listen to each other and, for those with power (i.e. the media), to hold those with influence to account.

The challenge is to overturn 40 years of negative reporting on the European Union. There is a dearth of knowledge about the EU (simply listen to some of James O'Brien's callers), but people aren't stupid, they are just misinformed. If they feel attacked, they will double down in their support for Leave.

I am also aware of how abusive many Leavers can be, and I certainly don't think we should accept abuse. However, if other Leavers are willing to engage in a good faith debate, then we should do what we can to present our strongest case and hope we can change their minds.

## Lance

Caught up in the optimism of the Leave campaign, Lance from Swansea, Wales, ended up voting Leave in 2016. He now considers most of this was lies and has changed his mind. He has become a RemainerNow and wants another vote.

*First published in January 2019.*

I voted Leave.
I too fell for the lies. I believed the ludicrous idea that Britain could rule the waves. That the European Union needed us more than we needed them, that we would get a better deal than we have and that we held all the cards.
I was wrong.
Sorry.
It was a head of heart vote, and I went with heart. Never again!
I started having doubts a few days after, especially when all the promises were rescinded. But it is Chequers that did it for me. As soon as it was written down it was clear that Brexit was simply impossible.

Most importantly, it was James O'Brien's LBC show that brought evidence and facts to the argument. Then, from James O'Brien, I found the podcasts of Remainiacs and Ian Dunt. Femi and OFOC have also done a sterling work and helped me see the errors of my ways.
The more I was listening to counter-arguments the more I understood I had fallen for the lies and unlawfulness of those Brexiters, out for themselves.

It is clear that many Leave voters have changed their mind and are #RemainerNow, which is why it is important too for democracy that we get a People's Vote now

## Bradley

Bradley, from Yorkshire, voted Leave in protest against Cameron's Government and the London-centric political class. When he realised that Brexit would be a disaster for the North East, he changed his mind. A Remainer-Now, he thinks a People's Vote is the only logical democratic solution.

If David Cameron thought for a moment that, when casting their votes in the 2016 Referendum, voters would base their choice purely upon issues relating to the EU, he was very wide of the mark.

I would love to claim that I cast my vote in a rational and disciplined manner, confining myself solely to consideration of the merits or otherwise of the UK's membership of the EU — but that would be a fib.

Instead, I was one of those who used the opportunity provided by Mr Cameron to register a protest against a Government (and indeed, a political class) who didn't appear to care for the needs and concerns of the North East of England (where I live) or any other region of the UK outside London for that matter.

To be honest, I didn't think that Leave had any chance of prevailing and I was thus both surprised and a little worried when I heard the result of the vote. Not normally given to retrospection, I found myself analysing the reasons why I had voted Leave.

I realised that, as well as registering a protest against the London-centricity of the political class, I had also used my vote as an adverse reaction to a number of advocates for the Remain side who appeared to be incapable of empathising with the genuine concerns of large numbers of Leave voters (in respect of immigration and regional economic development) and who appeared to assume that the result of the Referendum was a foregone conclusion and that consequently they didn't really need to try very hard to win-over Leave supporters (whom they appeared to view as 'unsophisticated uneducated provincials').

As time has moved on and as the spectral promises made by the leaders of the Leave campaign have evaporated and been replaced by objective evidence-based facts, I have realised that my region — the North East of England — stands to gain nothing and lose so much if the UK leaves the EU.

Do I regret casting my vote for Leave in 2016 ? Not only do I regret it but I am embarrassed by it. A mature, reasonably intelligent chap should not have based a decision to vote in a certain way in a crucial vote, on issues which were irrelevant and distracting, but I did! And I know that others to whom I have spoken within my area did likewise and now regret their decision just as much as I do.

I believe that, in the light of the impasse that currently exists, the democratic way out of that impasse is to hold a further Referendum. Those who argue that the British People have already had their say back in 2016 are clearly not taking into account the hundreds of thousands of people who have achieved the age of majority in the past 29 months and thus joined the electorate and the thousands of people who are no longer members of the electorate (either because they have passed away or emigrated). The 'British People' is not an unchanging entity, it is a dynamic group which has changed massively since the 2016 Referendum.

And there are many like me who did vote in 2016, but who have now changed their minds in the light of emerging evidence. The 'British People' who will be affected by the UK remaining in or leaving the EU in 2019 are the people whose 'will' should be taken into account, their futures should not be determined by the votes cast by a very differently constituted group 29 months ago. A People's Vote is the only logical democratic solution.

## Jessica

Like 17.4 million voters, Jessica voted Leave in 2016, but she has since realised how badly Brexit has been handled by Government and Theresa May. She is a Remainer now. She thinks we should be building bridges not walls and wants a People's Vote.

I voted Leave for a few reasons.

One reason being that I had close friends who owned businesses, who told me that tough regulations from the EU made it really hard for small businesses like theirs to thrive and that, if Brexit happened, they would be able to trade with countries outside of the EU.

I myself was, at the time, in the process of starting my own business, and was told if Brexit happened there would be fewer regulations and a cheaper VAT. I was told that by a student of economics, so I trusted their opinion. But it would appear now that that was not accurate because it seems that VAT could rise after Brexit.

The reason I have changed my mind is because of the amount of misinformation that was around at the time of the vote and that has been around since too.

Also, the way it has been handled since by the government is appalling. Nothing was planned. They have had two years to come up with a deal and it feels like they have just thrown something together at the last minute.

I have absolutely no faith in our government or Theresa May, and I am actually fearful of a No-Deal Brexit.

I do think a lot of Leave voters have been misrepresented though. I am sick of hearing how we are all some kind of uneducated racists who did not know what we were voting for.

I am sure that's true of a lot of people, but people like me voted the way they did because they thought it would help the country. I am educated, I was at Uni at the time and I am fully supportive of immigration, I donate to refugee charities regularly. So, I think it is unfair to generalise.

Brexit didn't have to be the big shambles it has been, if it had been executed properly, things could have been different. But, as it goes, it is a big mess and a joke, and I think it will be detrimental to our country.

There is no doubt that the EU is flawed in some ways, as is any governed system. I think that, while there are issues, Brexit is not the cure. We should have negotiated with them, voted to change things we were unhappy with.

There has always been a lot of debate and fighting between the UK and the EU (there's a fascinating article about it on History.com). But I think we have given up on them too soon. We should be building bridges not walls.

## Pauline

Pauline, from Durham, didn't vote in 2016. She felt ill-equipped to make such a decision. Things have changed since and, a Remainer Now, she wants another chance and would choose to vote Remain.

I am a #RemainerNow.
I didn't vote in the 2016 referendum as I was recovering from a stroke, but also because I didn't think it affected me.
I wasn't really 'into' politics, so I didn't know what I was voting on.
I have spent the last year or so educating myself as much as possible (even looking at modern history and economics) to gain a better insight.

I have yet to come across a single shred of evidence, or even an opinion (and I have listened to and read MANY — from all sides of the debate), that would lead me to believe that leaving the European Union would be of any benefit to me, or the UK as a whole.

I am at an age now where this decision may not have much impact on my path in life anymore, but it will certainly affect the life opportunities of my children. They are not old enough to vote, so I would be voting with them in mind, and given the chance, through a second referendum, I would 100% vote to Remain.

# Ayo

Ayo, from Hackney, voted Leave in 2016 without fully understanding the implications of voting to leave the EU, especially for his epileptic daughter. Fed up with the Brexiters' claims and lies, he is a Remainer Now and wants a People's Vote.

The thing is unless you are not looking at this situation objectively, there is no way you can say people haven't changed their mind — in either direction.

Ordinarily, I would say the vote happened, end of story. However, the Brexit outlined then, is NOT the Brexit we see today. Regardless if you voted Leave or Remain, we should all want a final say on what is actually done in our name.

I seriously do not understand the logic of the Conservatives. Why own Brexit?

Share the responsibility, the process, and the outcome of delivering Brexit. When we come to a concrete, signed, workable, detailed, deliverable solution. If that is miles away from what was promised, how on earth can you justify shoving it down our necks? If you put the reality to the people and they still want to leave then they can vote for it.

I am soooo fed up with the "17.4 million people... bla bla bla" narrative. For f*** sake, we are not all the same. Nigel Farage voted Leave (that should have been my clue). I voted Leave, but I hate every single thing he stands for. I didn't vote for this nonsense, I didn't fully understand the implications of voting to leave the EU.

Some people I met voted Leave and admitted afterwards they didn't even know we where part of the European Union before all this started. I am not joking!

I met many people who did not vote at all because they thought it had nothing to do with them, and they now desperately want a chance to cast a vote, this time understanding the specific issue that affects them.

My daughter has epilepsy. A few months ago, I asked her consultant what the deal was with her specific medication and Brexit. He told me that it is being stockpiled and that it "should be ok"... I didn't vote for Brexit so my daughter "should be ok".

I looked in his eyes. I could tell he wasn't sure.

I love this country. It is not perfect, but I was built here. My parents came from Nigeria in the 1980s, have built a business, employ five people. Immigration is not perfect, but its benefits outweigh its drawbacks, and we do have controls, we just don't use them — another thing I didn't know!

I am just fed up of all the blatant lies I hear day after day, week after week. This is not about winning or losing, this is about what is best for Britain as a whole.

I live here, my children live here. When I voted Leave I took a big dump on my door step.

We need a People's Vote to clean the shit up!

# Mario

Mario, a retired teacher, voted Leave in 2016. He did so as he was promised a Brexit deal and more money for the NHS. But now he considers his vote has been hijacked and, as a result, he has changed his mind. He is a Remainer Now.

*First published in June 2019.*

I voted Leave. I listened to the Leave politicians who promised all sorts of deals which sounded great. One in particular, Davis I think, said that we would have all our present material benefits with the added addition of not having to pay all that money into the EU. When I found out that was a lie I felt pretty stupid.

As stated I voted for a deal. Now I've been told that I didn't really vote for a deal, that I really voted to leave without a deal. My vote has been, to my mind, hijacked to mean something for which I did not intend it.

The mistake was all mine in this regard I have been told. Now my vote is being used in a way that was not intended. This is fine as this is democracy, I have been told. I didn't know that if one voted for a particular outcome someone, could represent that outcome as meaning a completely different outcome. I feel pretty stupid about that.

I voted for the extra money for the NHS that was promised on the side of the bus. We're giving all of this cash to the EU. Why not give it to the NHS? I've since been told that although one of these sentences followed the other that did not mean that the two sentences were in any way related. And further, the people who said this had no right to say it. I wondered, as these were public faces then why would they say these things? I feel pretty stupid about that.

I've always believed that in a democracy one listened to the arguments put forward by politicians. One read the manifesto. One deliberated, one came to a decision and one placed an X beside one's choice based on this well thought out democratic stratagem. I've since been told that I'm wrong about this. Including Piers Morgan on a recent Question Time.

Apparently the correct method is to ignore what the politicians say, ignore the manifesto, the last Tory manifesto for the GM promised a deal, and just read what's beside where you're going to place your X. As this space never held any information whatsoever, except Leave/Remain then it means that there had been really nothing to consider as "Leave means Leave." What Leave actually meant had been decided by others. Who these 'others' were and how they came to this definition of Leave I have not been able to find out.

I'm now 65 years old and have voted in this way for as long as I've been able to vote. Now I've found out that the proper way to vote is just have a look at the ballot paper and skip everything else. I feel pretty stupid.

I have other friends who voted Leave. We discussed this at length before the referendum and like me they wanted a good deal and voted along these lines. Or so we thought. Now I find out this was never the case. They knew all along there would be no deal, they always wanted out without a deal. During all of those conversations I must not have listened properly. I feel pretty stupid about that.

I don't know if everyone who voted Leave feels stupid. But there's one here.

## Sarah

Sarah from Christchurch voted Leave to express her anger at 'the establishment'. She has since changed her mind after seeing the government's shambolic negotiations. She is a RemainerNow and would like to have another say to vote to Remain.

*First published in June 2019.*

In October 2018, I faced-up to the realisation that I no longer thought the country should be leaving the EU. I say 'faced-up' to as no one likes to admit they had got such an important decision wrong, and some of my reasons for changing my views came from the way the Government was handling the negotiations, which came to light around that time.

I tweeted in October 2018 that I had made a mistake and, all things considered, I thought we should remain within the EU. @RemainerNow saw my message and made me aware of others who like me had changed their minds. I found this comforting as I had (and still have) a feeling of guilt over what I had done with my vote in June 2016.

As most people would do, I spent some time going over in my mind why I had voted Leave and how I feel now. Here are my thoughts:

To some extent, I bought into the "they need us more than we need them" statement that was frequently quoted, that we would be able to get a great deal as we were the fifth largest economy in the world and hugely important financially to the European Union.

Politicians, economic experts, financial experts, etc. on the Leave campaign told us that it would be easy to leave and to ignore the scaremongering from Remain.

Looking back, now I see that Remain led a very negative campaign aimed at discrediting Leave. How I wish they had done much less of this and concentrated on giving the public some facts detailing the benefits of our EU membership.

In the run-up to the referendum, I considered how I would vote. I had never really identified as European, and I was aware that my decision was going to come down to heart vs head.

On reflection, I know that my decision was based more on an emotional feeling rather than anything else. In particular, I remember the Obama speech, a few days before the referendum. It made me angry. The popular leader of the most powerful country in the world telling 'us' what to do. It reinforced what I was already thinking: we could make it on our own and whilst there would be some economic pain, it would all be worth it, in a few years.

I felt quite safe going with my heart as I never truly believed the vote would go that way, I stupidly believed in the polls giving Remain a consistent majority. I simply got to have my say and stick two fingers up at 'the establishment'.

Initially, when I heard the news of 'my win', I was happy.
By the Saturday after the vote, there was significant speculation that we would never actually leave as Parliament and the Civil Service simply wouldn't allow it. I was reassured by this and told my Remain-voting daughter not to worry.

Within weeks after the referendum, there were a few reports of Eastern European people in my local area being attacked, including children. I was horrified. Again, probably naively, I never anticipated that the vote would bring out such racism and hatred for those that don't appear to be white or British.

I am now genuinely worried about the numbers of EU and other foreign workers not staying in the UK. I am very aware of how much, for example, the NHS and the Healthcare system rely on foreign workers. Whilst they are not all from the EU, post-Brexit vote the environment has, to an extent, become hostile towards them. We need them here to support not only our services but also to pay into the tax system.

From what I can remember, around September last year, it was first reported that Leave negotiations weren't going well. I had naively assumed that thorough plans would have been put in place by the time we had even invoked Article 50 and that they would be progressing well given that we were leaving in March 2019. It transpired that all the trade deals that we had been promised by the Leave campaigners weren't actually so easy to get.

An issue that I had paid some attention to before the vote was that of security. Being part of the EU gave me a feeling of security and safety. I had listened to two interviews on national radio before the 2016 vote; both guests gave reassurances that we shouldn't worry about the sharing of information on suspected criminals, terrorists, etc. I also recall one interview where the Leave interviewee stated that we had probably the best intelligence in the world, and so the EU would be desperate to keep all means of sharing information open with us.

I have since come to understand that whilst they will still want to work very closely with us, we will no longer have access to the existing systems to do that. This concerns me greatly.

Another issue which only a small minority of the public were aware of before the referendum was that of the Irish Border. I grew up in Farnborough, next to Aldershot, and was surrounded by the Army. I am of an age where I can remember seeing the aftermath of both the Aldershot and Guildford bombings, and whilst there is no tangible evidence to think Brexit could reopen divisions in Ireland, had I have any understanding of the issues around the Irish Border, there is categorically no way I would have voted Leave.

I could write more, but I think I have said what I wanted to in terms of why I regret my vote to leave the European Union, and wish I could have the chance to have my say again.

# Lisa

This is Lisa from Wakefield in West Yorkshire. She voted Leave in the 2016 Referendum, but she regrets her vote and is a Remainer Now. She wants a People's Vote to have a final say on Brexit.

*First published in March 2019. | Updated in September 2019.*

I voted Leave but realise how I was lied to. So, I now believe the public should be allowed to change their minds, now they have more information on what Brexit will look like, and have a People's Vote.

I naively believed the lies and the now-known illegal Leave campaign. I have to say I feel really stupid, but I did believe the "they need us more than we need them" narrative, how easy it would be to negotiate a deal, the money that we pay in every year for the NHS, also immigration.

I'm not anti-immigration, I just think we should be able to control who comes here and how many.

I think I realised I had made a mistake over the last six to nine months when I saw how difficult the negotiations were, when they said it would be easy. I think I have realised that a lot of the Tory MPs have their own agenda and are self-serving.

They don't seem to care about what happens to the country as long as they get their way. I have realised also that when Vote Leave were found to have broken electoral law, I thought it was sneaky and not true democracy, but because the referendum was advisory only, no action as regards to reversing it can be taken.

Also, the fact that the government thinks it's ok for the same deal to be voted on numerous times in case MPs have changed their minds, but it's undemocratic for the public to have a vote in case we have changed our minds now that we have more information!

Contempt for the public I think!
When I voted, I did not vote for the shambles we have now!! It's a complete mess and a disgrace!! We have a government who has had a motion rejected with the highest amount of votes against them and that have been found in contempt of parliament.

I was very naive and should have done more research, but there were so many conflicting arguments it was hard to know what to believe. I have also been really worried about the future trade negotiations with the US. I don't trust this government to not give them access to the NHS.

I also worry about food regulations, employment laws and workers rights. I can't believe how gullible I have been. I am really sorry I didn't realise before I voted that if the type of Tories that want it, want it, it can only be bad for the rest of us.

I really have been very stupid!!!

I think that if the government thinks it's ok to bring the Withdrawal Agreement multiple times for a vote, in the hope that MPs will change their mind, then the public should have the chance to change their minds too and have a People's Vote.

I would like to change my vote as I feel it is only right, and democratic, especially as parliament have voted twice already on Theresa May's deal and maybe soon for a third time.

# Jen

Jen, a teacher from Southampton, voted Leave in 2016. She slowly started to see Brexit becoming nothing like what was promised to voters like her. She also understands the EU better now. Jen is a Remainer Now.

*First published in September 2019.*

I voted Leave, but I DID NOT vote for No-Deal. The concept of No-Deal did not even exist during the referendum!!

In 2016, it seemed to me that by voting Leave the UK would keep all the benefits of being in the European Union (Single Market/Freedom of Movement, etc.), but have less EU rules and more money. I am a teacher and a mother. I did not have the time to decipher what was a Vote Leave broadcast and what was not.

But then, I slowly started to see Brexit becoming nothing like what was promised. People, however, seemed to be blind to this fact just because they had 'won' and accepted the lies. If MPs in Government are telling me something, how am I supposed to know it is only an 'intention'?

This is not a football match. It is the future of a Nation and people's lives. In 2016, Britain said Leave. Now, after 3 years, we ACTUALLY know what 'Leave' means. I (we) know so much more now!

When the Leave/Cambridge Analytica scandal started to unravel I was horrified. Again Leave voters are either ignoring this or not bothered because they 'won'. It is not even about Leave vs Remain, it is about a fair and informed electorate and Democracy.

I wanted to find out what Leave voters would think if it were the other way round and Remain had broken the law to sway votes, promote lies and ultimately subvert Democracy. So, I maybe asked 200 people on Twitter, and so far 0 have responded.

What does that tell you?

Being free from EU control and laws was also a factor that made me voted Leave. Only after the vote did I find out how the EU Parliament actually works.

I am so annoyed with myself that I fell for the Leave fiction on Facebook and in the media. Especially after I saw this Twitter thread and could not believe it. All those EU rules Brexiters go mad about... There are actually just 72 laws that were forced on us, and they 100% benefit the UK! And every other EU law has been voted for by UK MEPs and passed by UK Ministers.

So much for the EU being undemocratic!

**Jamie**

The fascinating story of Jamie, who voted Leave in 2016, and went from wanting the UK to leave the EU without a deal to becoming a #Remainer-Now and now even supporting a People's Vote. Here he is correcting his own misguided tweets...

*First published in October 2019.*

• Jamie Thomas, is a musician who describes himself as "a Socialist and a Leaver transformed into a Remainer".
• He wrote and shared the following story on Twitter.
• It was turned into this article by the PMP Editorial Team to be fully readable.

This has probably been done before but basically, I am a #RemainerNow and I thought I would have a look through my old tweets out of curiosity and respond to them correcting myself, and pointing out how silly I was. So here goes.

8 Feb 2019 | "Verhofstadt is an elected Member of the European Parliament. Elected by whom exactly?"
Verhofstadt is an MEP. He was elected by the people of Belgium in the European Parliament elections.

18 March 2019 | "Both campaigns played dirty, and people can't say they weren't informed; the Remain campaign's strategy was to outline the worst case scenario – we may well be close to that scenario now but we voted as informed people. Anyone who wasn't informed in 2016 would be just as ignorant."
As has been revealed since by the Government's own data, the worst case scenario was right. But the Leave campaign dismissed it as 'Project Fear' and enough people believed them to affect the result. But now we have a chance to avoid that worst case scenario.

20 March 2019 | "We are leaving, Remain has been off the table since 2016."
No, it hasn't!!! I have changed my mind on this, and so many others have too. Just look at the polling for Leave vs Remain. If you leave Remain off

the ballot paper, you remove the ability for us to show we have changed our mind.

21 March 2019 | "If I put an offer on a house that half the country were campaigning to say, "Hey guy, don't buy that house, it might fall down", then I obviously really need a house. People voted Leave despite all the campaigning from the other side. Get real."
The house is now falling down and we have a chance to run away and get to safety.

21 March 2019 | "Three years is not a very long time ago."
Three years is clearly long enough for the country to change its mind (see polling) and while I still believe revoking Article 50 is a bad idea, having a confirmatory referendum between a deal and Remain is THE MOST democratic solution to this problem.

23 March 2019 | "We had a referendum, that was our chance to make our views known. You should be grateful we are allowed to have petitions and protests in the first place. Some people don't have that privilege."
What an awful tweet. Putting aside the plain rudeness, I seem to be implying that once our votes have been recorded we cannot change our minds. We are now careering towards something we don't want, because we voted for it with little correct info.

23 March 2019 | "We were presented with worst case scenarios by the Remain campaign before the referendum took place. People knew what they were voting for. We were told this was a once-in-a-generation thing and that there would be no second referendum. Not to mention how undemocratic it would be."
A second referendum with a Deal vs Remain would be MORE DEMOCRATIC. Why? Once we have a defined Leave option, there won't be any "we'll get the best deal ever" rubbish. A simple choice between two defined options.

23 March 2019 | "Those who can vote but choose not to forfeit their right to complain about the result. While you're correct about how referendums aren't binding, it would diminish the importance of referendums in the future by quite a lot if the result were to be ignored."
But the result has not been ignored, that is why successive Prime Ministers and governments have attempted to negotiate a deal with the EU that can pass through Parliament. It is still OK to ask "Now that we have a defined Leave option, is this what you want?"

23 March 2019 | "If their fears and concerns are stupid then it isn't as bad."
This is a stupid and ignorant tweet, and I am sorry.


10 April 2019 | "Sure it has a higher number in that image than the other options, but the Leave option has been split into three. If the referendum were between those three options, it would make more sense. We already voted to leave, a second referendum should be about how."
Sure, if you add up those three options then the Leave vote is larger than the Remain vote, but in the end if we leave we're only going to leave with ONE of those options, none of which can get a majority over Remain.

25 April 2019 | "If there is an option to remain, or it is not specified, they are losing my vote to the Brexit Party."
I did end up voting for the Brexit Party in the EU elections. Massively regret that. I don't think I'm the only one who did it. Now, I'm annoyed at Labour for not yet deciding to CAMPAIGN FOR Remain in their second referendum. How things have changed...

30 April 2019 | "It's only right that Labour means Leave – I'm glad that the party I support has given clarity that it does in fact see sense."
Wrong, wrong, wrong, wrong, wrong, wrong, wrong. Labour is the only main party that will give the public a final say and that is huge. That is sensible. If Labour meant Leave I would be politically homeless.

I guess the point of this thread is that it's okay to change your mind. At the beginning of this year I wanted to leave the EU without a deal and now I am a Remainer in full. I will be going to the People's Vote March in London next week.
People are asking what made me change my mind: using Twitter more regularly. I wanted to get balanced political news, so I followed people from both sides of the argument and I quite rapidly came around.

For a bit towards June kind of time I supported Brexit mainly for 'democratic' reasons just because it won the referendum, so it was sort of an empty support by that time. I think the turning point was the Tory leadership contest and He Who Shall Not Be Elected entering Number 10.

# Claire

Claire voted Leave in 2016. She immediately regretted her vote when she realised she had played into the hands of people who care not one jot about the UK's best interest. A Remainer Now, she would proudly vote Remain in a second referendum.

*First published in October 2019.*

I believed the lies of having more money for the NHS and public funding, and wanted to see a fairer spread of wealth and skills across country, particularly in areas where industry had gone overseas.

I also wanted to put a sting in rising house/rental prices which were already becoming well out of reach and I thought that it might actually help the Eurozone, knowing high youth-unemployment in EU countries was causing fractured communities and economic issues there.

Also, rising stress levels, mental health, loneliness, fast cheap fashion and single-use plastic were also a concern and I was growing increasingly worried for the environment, the pollution and exploitation our western consumer habits were having on other countries.

With all these concerns, I thought that this vote could possibly be the catalyst that was needed to help promote real social change.

Mostly though, I felt not enough time or information was provided to make a sufficient argument for either side and when I looked to the Remain side, I felt insulted by "Project Fear" and didn't like being told how to vote. I also voted partly out of protest at this.

My understanding from Leave was that we would remain in the single market and still retain some EU benefits – although of course it wasn't clear which ones. However, if this is what was needed to help bring about true systemic change, then maybe this was it…

I was also under the impression from Leave that once a new deal had been negotiated we would get the chance to vote on the new deal or keep things as is, and continue to push for reform from inside the EU, so that we could better improve things for all.

Now I know my frustrations were more to do with the western capitalist system we currently live in, and I quickly regretted my vote once events unfolded and the lies spilled out, and the idea of a "Hard" Brexit came about, especially after the Cambridge Analytica scandal.

I felt sick and anxious when I realised we had played into the hands of the very people who care more about their own political careers, power plays and lining their own pockets, than the people they are supposed to protect, and that anxiety still hasn't gone away.

I certainly did not vote for this so-called "Hard Brexit" and to be stuck on this island with no access to the rest of the continent, higher purchase prices or separate visas, and advantage for bankers, the rich getting richer and the poorer staying poor…

I fear for the future of this country, the division and xenophobia it's caused and the lack of talent and investment we are now losing to overseas, every day. But at least one positive is that we have all learnt a whole lot more facts about the situation for both sides.

I now realise that a lot of the home issues are a result of our own government not taking action and not the EU. They already had many of the powers to deal with the issues often complained about, our government just chose not to do anything about them. I also fear there are a lot of things this government is deliberately not doing, and the thought of no longer having any EU protection from that worries me.

I have always been pro-European and wish that our government and media were not so biased, and spent more time informing us of the positives of the EU instead, and what we are paying into and the good work that is being done even across the UK alone.

I believe other countries are much better educated on these facts and therefore hold a much better view of the EU than we do because of this.

I also feel that being in the EU is important for continuing peace, prosperity and collaboration of ideas, academia and science, conservation of nature and protecting the planet – and I honestly hope the UK can still continue to be a part of it somehow, and that the real reforms are done now within our own government system to finally tackle the corruption, inequality and lack of funding for public services in this country, so we can all move forward together.

Knowing what I know now, I would vote Remain with a bold and proud cross on that ballot sheet.

# Jane

Jane, a Northerner living in Oxford, voted Leave in 2016. As her life started to improve, she realised she had fallen for Vote Leave's tricks. She has since decided to speak up and has become a Remainer Now who is campaigning for a People's Vote.

*First published in December 2019.*

I voted Leave but I now feel lied to and conned. I deeply regret this decision. I now believe that a People's Vote is the only sensible route with ALL the facts presented to the electorate!

Why did I vote Leave? Why do I advocate for a People's Vote?
I am a Northerner who has been living in Oxford for the last 19 years. I am very lucky to live here notwithstanding the cost of high rents, etc.

I found myself homeless twice. Once was when my daughter was only 3 years old. We slept on my friends living room floor for 6 weeks, before Social Services felt obliged to step in and help with locating an amenable landlord. The Council would not help. I got lucky... I could see how private landlords were profiting from buying their previous social housing.

I could see how my friends from back home (Accrington, Blackburn, Burnley) were forgotten. Their towns feel like ghost towns from shop closures, underinvestment, unemployment and dare I say it but whole areas were being "ghettoised" by immigration and refugees.

These small towns became a dumping ground because of cheap rents. It was a protest vote against capitalists and the Tories.

I did not buy into the Boris bus by the way. Unfortunately, I realise I bought into the rhetoric that these problems were because of immigration rather than austerity politics and blaming the 'other'.

I have since educated myself and feel deeply ashamed about my decision. I am also debating with other people and friends to change their minds. I fell for the oldest trick in the book: to divide people based on their differences. Life is hopeful these days.

I have returned to university and I am an undergraduate student in Sociology and Politics. My daughter is also studying A-Level Sociology and intends to do this as a degree in a couple of years time. I intend to retrain as a teacher and make right the wrongs I have been a part of.

It is interesting to note that Social Sciences, particularly Politics, has had a remarkable uptake. No coincidence.
I have noticed that those I know personally, who are still very much for Brexit, have some common threads:
◦ Refusal to look at the facts explained to them;
◦ Benefited from austerity;
◦ Benefited from asset stripping (former council houses).
There is a real sense of the "I'm all right Jack," and no thought for inequalities and social justice.

AND, I have not felt so encouraged and passionate about Labour since the John Smith days!

I NEVER forget who I am, or where I am from. I am proud to be a Northerner. I ask the question all the time about what it is to be a Northerner: to speak out, to say it how it is, big gob and big heart. AND to say it's "cowd out here".
My story is only one part of many others who feel ignored and disregarded.

# Emma

Emma from Southend-on-Sea voted Leave in 2016 but she is a Remainer Now. She wrote a letter to her MP asking him to protect EU citizens and their families after Parliament voted down an amendment that would have prevented a Windrush 2.0.

*First published in January 2020.*

I am writing in regard to the Amendment that was voted down yesterday regarding EU/EEA citizens and their dependants having an automatic status as promised by the Prime Minister during the 2016 referendum campaign.
I am so worried and scared for people who live here who may be unable to apply for the settled status scheme and are vulnerable.
It hurts so much as a mum to think that children and families are still in limbo and it tears me in two.
Please help them.
I am a nobody but please do everything you can to help them. They didn't even get a vote or say in this.

As you know, I have two boys with low functioning autism and I know already some families like mine who have had to leave which has caused them all so much distress and fear.
Please protect EU Citizens in the UK and British In Europe. Please do everything you can.
I would suggest the best way for everyone to come together on peace, re-gardless of view, is to put people first and show how much we care about people as a nation.
I love our country and all its people. People who love our country have my respect and I want the best for them and indeed us all. If you know of anything I can do, please tell me.
I voted Leave in 2016 but I never voted or thought this would happen. Please help them.

## PART FOUR
## Moving Forward


**RemainerNow Mission Statement from Andy**

Many people have asked, given the fact that Brexit now cannot be prevented, is the RemainerNow 'campaign' going to continue? If so, what is the point?

*First published in January 2020*


In short, yes, it will continue (albeit it less intensely), and yes, there is a point.

When the @RemainerNow Twitter account was set up in December 2017 it was done so as a result of fear about the direction of the country. It was done due to grave concerns of the lack of consideration the Government appeared to be giving to the impact of its Brexit decisions and due to a feeling of being totally fed up with the Government pretending it had an overwhelming mandate to pursue Brexit, however it pleased.

It was decided that a good way to contribute to the debate was to highlight that, as well as those who voted Remain, many people who voted Leave did not agree with what was being done in their name.

At that time the People's Vote campaign did not even exist (it was not founded until April 2018) and the idea of stopping Brexit was very much a fringe view. Now, things changed over the course of the two years that followed, and at a couple of points in 2019 it looked like we were quite close to achieving a second referendum. If this had happened we maintain our belief that the voices of the thousands of people we engaged with that voted Leave (or abstained) and changed their minds could well have become pivotal.

It was with the changing sands in the political situation that this "campaign" grew from one person tweeting whilst commuting to and from work, to a multi-channel and real-life campaign run by a team of six for us, all covering different aspects (in our spare time) including a full-time campaign manager (thanks to support from crowdfunds).

Now sadly, as we know, the goal of achieving a Final Say/People's Vote on Brexit is no longer achievable. Whilst we maintain it is not in the country's interests, we must accept that Brexit (at least legally) is inevitable on 31 January. But, for the record, we firmly believe the Brexit being pursued by this new Government is not happening because this path has the support of the majority of this country, but instead it is because the Government gained a majority following a general election campaign that: (a) lacked honesty on the trade-offs ahead (especially on Brexit), (b) where Brexit was not necessarily the main issue driving many voters, and (c) where our flawed electoral system continues to allow a sizeable parliamentary majority on a minority of the popular vote.

Given the situation the country is now in, the RemainerNow campaign will continue to be here, though not in the same form as before. Our overall activity will decrease (as we lose our full-time staff-member, some volunteers drop away and others focus more on home life) but we hope to be effective in what we do, especially as now that we are no longer faced with constant urgency to act (such as chasing bills and amendments through the Commons on an almost weekly basis).

In many ways, we are not in a dissimilar position now to where it seemed we were in December 2017, and the same desire to hold this Brexit government to account on which this initiative started, remains. Accordingly, whilst we will not be pushing any immediate quest to rejoin the EU (mainly as we do not consider this the best strategy at this time – but never say never), we do think there is a need for this campaign and network going forward.

Our plans for 2020 are therefore:

1. To continue to highlight any occasions where this government, and those others pursuing Brexit, fail to live up to the promises that they have made to the public (both in 2016 and more recently) on what Brexit will mean. We must #HoldThemToAccount.

2. As Brexit will not be "done" by any stretch of the imagination on 31 January 2020, we will assist all those opposing this Government's current plans and push to at least mitigate the (likely) negative effects of Brexit. This will include doing our best to try and advocate the need to keep close Single Market alignment and doing what we can to help protect the rights of EU citizens in the UK, and the British in Europe, to provide certainty for their futures.

3. To help champion other progressive causes and cross-party working that we think are vital for the future of this country, including coming battles on climate change, tackling homelessness and the need for constitutional and voting reform.

4. Maintain our network of all those people who are RemainerNow and, should they wish, do our best to help share their stories/help publish articles, or alternatively to work with any other campaigns/journalists/MPs who think hearing from those who changed their minds on Brexit is worthwhile.

5. To continue to be a forum for any new RemainerNow. We have seen people change their minds at virtually every stage of the campaign and expect this to continue. If we are correct that the reality of Brexit will be very different from what is promised, we want to be here to give those new 'RemainerNow' people a voice (we do not expect this to be instant but that there may be many in the latter half of the year when the wider public become clearer on the complexities and trade-offs of "Getting Brexit Done").

If this approach is one you can support, please do continue following us on our various platforms and also encourage other like-minded individuals who do not know about us yet to join us on social media or our website.

**Recommended Further reading**

Led by Donkeys - How four friends with a ladder took on Brexit
James O'brien - How to be Right in a World Gone Wrong
Gavin Esler - Brexit without the bullshit
Elena Remigi - In Limbo & In Limbo 2
David Cameron - For the record
Christopher Bartram - Brexit: What the Hell happened?
John Bercow - Unspeakable
Nick Clegg - How to Stop Brexit (And Make Britain Great Again)

## Acknowledgements

First of all it is important to pay tribute to the founding members of the Re-mainerNow campaign. Andy, who is our leader and founder, is a man of great talent, passion and of a forgiving nature. I have told him many times and will say once more: Thank you for giving us a voice! Thank you for fuelling our fire and giving us the skills and confidence we needed to go out into one of the most derisive situations in our modern history and attempt to make a difference.

Victoria, our campaign manager, approached Andy in the early days and offered her skills and experience. If Andy is the Father of the campaign, Victoria is undoubtably its mother. She has always been kind and supportive with a presence that can calm a march and rally a dispirited meeting.

I could go on naming individuals in the campaign but that would require another book to fit in. Instead allow me to thank followers and activists as a group for their support and continued action. Thank you to all those MP's and MEP's who have championed us throughout this journey.

Thank you to PMP Magazine for helping us get our stories out to a new audience. Visit them on their website: pmp-magazine.com

Finally, I would like to thank my wonderful fiancé, Ellie. She has continued to support me through and through and continues to do so. Without her, I could have never done what I have, nor do what I'm about to start. She has my eternal thanks and love.

Printed in Great Britain
by Amazon

83174116R00072